ALAN TURING

A LIFE STORY

Joanna Nadin

Illustrated by **Sarah Papworth**

■SCHOLASTIC

For Ben and Zac, who understand maths,
and why Alan mattered.

Published in the UK by Scholastic Children's Books, 2020
Euston House, 24 Eversholt Street, London, NW1 1DB
A division of Scholastic Limited

London ~ New York ~ Toronto ~ Sydney ~ Auckland
Mexico City ~ New Delhi ~ Hong Kong

Text © Joanna Nadin, 2020
Illustrations by Sarah Papworth

ISBN 978 1407 19319 9

A CIP catalogue record for this book is available from the British Library.

Printed and bound by CPI Group (UK) Ltd, Croydon, CR0 4YY

Papers used by Scholastic Children's Books are made from woods grown in
sustainable forests.

2 4 6 8 10 9 7 5 3 1

www.scholastic.co.uk

CONTENTS

INTRODUCTION

Meet Alan Turing: genius mathematician, heroic wartime codebreaker, the founder of computing and gay rights icon. You see, this man didn't just do one brilliant thing in his lifetime – he racked up a whole list of them.

He was the man who, years before anyone had even imagined such a machine, came up with the theory that would pave the way for the modern computer. He also came up with what we now know as "artificial intelligence", foreseeing a day when computers would not just outwit humans at chess, but be able to imitate them so well they might fool other humans. Next he turned his maths brilliance to the world of biology to explain the appearance of what's known as the Fibonacci sequence in leaves, and why leopards got their spots. And he still found the time to keep up his top level long-distance running, only just missing out on representing Britain at the 1948 Olympics.

But best of all, his theories cracked the "impossible" Enigma encryption machine in World War Two, helping British intelligence get one step ahead of German attacks, and saving millions of lives in the process. All this from a boy whose school reports had written him off as "not very good" and "a very grubby person".

What makes his story even more extraordinary is that these incredible achievements went virtually unrecognized in his own lifetime. Instead of being grateful, the government treated him as a danger to society and he died not a hero, but in disgrace. Thankfully, that's all changed now, and Alan Turing's name is synonymous with codebreaking as well as computing, and not just in Britain but around the whole world.

This is the story of how Alan went from struggling schoolboy to gifted and talented academic to wartime hero to computer innovator. It's an extraordinary story, but then his was an extraordinary life.

FIBONACCI SEQUENCE

The Fibonacci sequence is the series of numbers **0, 1, 1, 2, 3, 5, 8, 13, 21, 34** and so on. The next number is made by adding together the two previous numbers.

It can be seen throughout nature – in the patterns of sunflower seeds, the distinct shape of pinecones, the number of petals on some flowers, and elsewhere.

TURING'S BRITAIN

Before we meet Alan, it's worth knowing a little about what life was like at the turn of the twentieth century.

Forget computer games and tablets, and even TV. Back then people were lucky to even have a telephone. Cars were few and far between, and the aeroplane had only just been invented. Instead, people used trains, boats, horses or bicycles to get around, or they just saddled up "Shanks's pony" (which meant walking).

Toys existed of course. There were board games and balls, as well as toy guns. But many children went without or made their own fun. One thing was the same though: school, which was compulsory even in those days, but only until you were twelve (although lots of children left long before that to start work). Everything was much stricter too, and school masters often punished children by caning them or beating them with a slipper (this was even legal). Lessons were different too, with an emphasis on traditional subjects like Latin and Greek rather than science and maths.

Adults didn't have it easy either. Few women went to university or worked in high-powered jobs and, along with working-class men, they couldn't vote. Although Queen Victoria died in 1901, strict Victorian values lingered, dictating what people should and shouldn't say, do and wear.

Another important difference back then was that Britain wasn't just Scotland, Wales and England but had its own "empire". That meant it ruled lots of other places, including Canada, Australia, parts of Africa and India. By 1912, the Empire stretched to over 400 million people – nearly a quarter of the world's population. Despite this power, Britain was on the brink of war with Germany.

This was the world Alan Mathison Turing was born into on 23 June 1912.

I think it's time to meet him.

VICTORIAN VALUES

Victorian values dictated that children should be "seen and not heard"; in other words, they should never answer adults back. Women were expected to cover up at all times – no trousers for them! And everyone had to be polite at all times.

THE SCRUFFY SCHOOLBOY

All in the Family

Alan Turing's life was fairly extraordinary from the day he was born.

His mother, Ethel Sara Stoney (who later began going by just Sara), was highly educated, which was unusual for a woman at that time. She attended Cheltenham Ladies' College as well as the famous Sorbonne in Paris for university.

In fact, the Stoney family were rather an exceptional lot, making a mark in the fields of mathematics and science, where Alan was to find his passion and later fame. Alan's distant cousin, George Johnstone Stoney, who died the year before Alan was born, had been a scientist and was best known for coining the word "electron". Determined that his daughters should be as well-educated as their brothers, George sent

Edith Anne to Cambridge to study maths. She later lectured in physics and became president of the Association of Science Teachers. Meanwhile, her sister, Florence Ada, became a consultant radiologist who served in World War One and was awarded the Admiralty Star as well as an OBE. George's brother, who went by the unlikely name of Bindon Blood Stoney, was a successful railway engineer and became known as the "father of Irish concrete". Another Stoney, Edward Waller, became the chief engineer in Madras, India and was awarded the rather wordy title of Companion of the Order of the Indian Empire.

Edward was Ethel's father – Alan's grandfather – and it was there, in Madras, that she first met a young civil servant called Julius Turing.

An Unusual Arrangement

Julius and Ethel married in India in 1907. A year later, Ethel gave birth to their first son, John Ferrier, in Madras, where she herself had been born. In fact, it seems almost an accident that Alan was born in Britain at all. In 1912, Julius and Ethel brought John back to England on what was called "extended leave" – a sort of long holiday for people who worked abroad. Ethel was pregnant at the time, and a few months later, on 23 June, in Warrington Lodge Nursing Home in Little Venice in London, they welcomed Alan into the world.

Then, Julius's leave at an end, Alan's parents returned to Madras as expected; Julius first and Ethel a few months later. What was not expected, at least not by us today, is that they left their small boys, Alan and John, behind in England. This can't have been an easy decision to make but, not long before this, John had contracted the disease dysentery from infected cows' milk, and become seriously ill with diarrhoea and vomiting, losing a dangerous amount of weight. Ethel was scared of it happening again and so, rather than risk the same fate for either of the boys, she handed them over to a Mr and Mrs Ward, who became the boys' foster parents for the next few years.

A BLUE PLAQUE

Warrington Lodge in Little Venice, where Alan was born, is now the Colonnade Hotel. Alan is honoured by a blue plaque, which mark the English residences of some of the world's most important people, while another famous former resident, Sigmund Freud, has the best suite named after him.

Early Promise

The Wards lived in a rambling house called Baston Lodge in St Leonards-on-Sea, on the south coast of England. It was a busy home – they had four daughters of their own and an ever-changing roster of other foster children, including, at times, the Turings' cousins. The nursery, where Alan spent his time as a baby, was run by a formidable woman called Nanny Thompson, who stood for no nonsense. Despite this, Alan was happy enough here in the early days, playing with his brother and cousins, avoiding the Wards' daughter Joan (whom Alan thought was a "tyrant"), and seeing his parents when they returned for holidays. Mrs Ward found his lack of interest in guns and swords odd for a boy. Alan, it seems, much preferred books.

He was a bright child from the off, teaching himself to read and even inventing his own words:

"Greasicle" referred to the way a candle flickered or guttered in the wind.

"Quockling" was the noise made by seagulls fighting over food.

"Squaddy" described a shape that was a combination of squat and square.

It's obvious now that Alan had a gift for maths and science from a very early age. According to his mother, he was fascinated by numbers before he could even read and would study them wherever they appeared – on lamp posts, for example. Later, having been taught how to find the square root of a number, he worked out for himself how to find the cube root. He also conducted experiments and even wrote his own guide to the microscope, aged seven. This turned out to be a very short read, consisting only of the words,

"FIRST YOU MUST SEE THAT THE LITE IS RITE."

Despite this intelligence and aptitude, he struggled with some things the rest of us take for granted. He was always messy, for example; his shirt was often hanging out with hair sticking up every which way. He couldn't tell his left from right and used a red dot on his left thumb to help him remember, which he called his "knowing" spot. Nor could he fathom the calendar and didn't seem to understand that Christmas always fell on the same date. He even took to planting broken toy soldiers in the ground, hoping they would grow.

But he was an honest boy, determined to tell the truth above everything. When his mother asked if he would be good while she was away, he replied that he would, but that sometimes he would forget. It was this absolute honesty that was to cause him enormous trouble later in life.

Those days were still in the distant future though. First, there was school to get through. And, while he may have been bright, school wasn't necessarily easy or fun. Not in those days, and not if you had a tendency to be a scruffy sort of boy.

Alan and John later moved to other foster parents – The Meyers – in Hertfordshire.

A young
Alan
Turing

The Reluctant Schoolboy

At the age of nine, Alan was sent to join his brother at boarding school in Sussex, a decision he was not initially happy with at all – his mother remembers him running after the car when she dropped him off, arms wide and shouting. Shout he might well have. Because, instead of being left to his own devices – free to study science and his other love, nature – he now had to follow a strict curriculum, as well as a lot of rules.

Hazelhurst Preparatory School was small – it only had around forty boys, all of whom were being "prepared" – hence the name – for the Common Entrance Exam to get into public school (sometimes known as private school). This meant lessons in Latin, English, French, history, geography, scripture (the Bible) and maths, but a notable lack of science. Science, back then, wasn't rated very highly at private school at all, or in fact any school – it wasn't even part of the compulsory curriculum until 1988. Sport and the classics were seen as far more important, especially for boys of Alan's social class.

Origami

Still, Alan got by, in his own way. First, he started a craze for origami, making paper boats, paper hats, paper donkeys and even paper kettles. He also became obsessed with maps, managing to beat his older brother by a wide margin in a geography exam (much to John's shame, one suspects). He invented his own fountain pen, too, using it to write home in his weekly letters about another invention he hoped to make: his own typewriter. Although "home", as he knew it, was rather a moveable concept.

France

In 1924, when Alan was twelve, his father Julius stormed out of his job in India in a huff when someone he didn't rate very highly was promoted above him. In order to avoid paying a massive tax bill, the Turings took up residence on the north coast of France instead of moving back to England. This meant that holidays were spent on the beaches at Dinard, or more commonly for Alan, in the cellar below their house, conducting chemistry experiments. Despite the lack of study at school, Alan's fascination with science hadn't waned at all and he was even given private lessons by a friend of the family – Mr Rolf, a science master at Sherborne School.

This was to prove pivotal.

The time was coming for Alan to take the Common Entrance Exam and, up until this point, it had been assumed he would join John, who was already at Marlborough College. But John, knowing how Alan struggled with sport and Latin, which were very much the focus at Marlborough College, begged his mother to find Alan a different school. She chose Mr Rolf's school, Sherborne, in Dorset. And a new chapter in Alan's life began.

A Flying Start

Alan's first day at Sherborne marked him out as exceptional – some might say strange – from the very start.

However, the Turings were unaware that the day Alan set off from France by ferry for Southampton, England was in the middle of a general strike. This meant that no passenger trains were running at all (only the "milk trains", which took raw milk to be pasteurised in food-processing plants). When he found this out, instead of worrying or waiting for help, fourteen-year-old Alan decided to cycle the whole sixty miles to Dorset instead. Leaving his luggage at the station, and having bought himself an apple and a map, he rode through the New Forest, staying the night at a rather flash hotel in Blandford Forum, before finishing the last few miles to Sherborne the next morning.

This was astounding behaviour for a boy of his age and class, and unsurprisingly made the local paper. It was also a great story to spread around school, and he was almost a hero for the first few weeks.

That, however, quickly changed.

Public schools, especially boarding schools, were notorious in those days for being brutal. Teachers – or "masters" as they were known – regularly used corporal punishment like the cane, the ruler and the slipper. Even the students joined in with the bullying, forcing new boys to go through humiliating initiation ceremonies and submit to "fagging", which effectively meant being a slave to the older boys. That first term, poor Alan was made to sing in front of everyone, and then, worse, kicked up and down the day room in a rubbish basket. Later he was trapped under floorboards as well, which must have been a terrifying experience. His interest in chemistry was seen as "swottish" and his dislike of PE or games as wimpy. He was also considered "dirty", with his hair sticking out, his buttons done up wrong and perpetual ink stains.

Alan, frankly, did not fit in.

FOUCAULT'S PENDULUM

One act that did amuse some boys was when Alan set up an enormous "Foucault's pendulum" above a stairwell.

Named after the French physicist, Léon Foucault, the pendulum consists of a large weight attached to a long string, which swings back and forth and back and forth, slowly turning a full circle, proving that the Earth rotates.

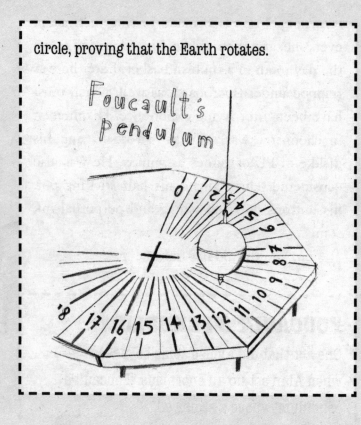

Foucault's pendulum

"Could Do Better"

Alan wasn't hugely favoured by the masters, as well as the students. Despite Alan's keenness and ability, they seemed far more concerned with his scruffiness and admittedly appalling handwriting. While maths and science were finally on the curriculum, Alan seems to have been bored by the elementary nature of classes and preferred to conduct his own experiments out of class, much to the anger of the masters. Similarly he was caught doing maths in a religious education class and his lack of interest in Latin – still considered key to a "proper" education – provoked one master (a Mr Bensly) to offer a billion pounds to charity if Alan could pass his exam.

It's no surprise that his school reports make for fascinating reading:

SUMMER TERM, 1926
House report: he's a very grubby person at times.

MICHAELMAS TERM, 1926
Maths: he is still very untidy. He must try to improve in this respect.

LENT TERM, 1927
House report: he is frankly not one who fits comfortably for himself into the ordinary life of the place.

And they only got worse:

SUMMER TERM, 1927

Maths: not very good… His work is dirty.

House Report: he is mistaken in acting as if idleness and indifference will procure release from uncongenial subjects.

One master even complained about finding Alan conducting an experiment on his own at night.

MICHAELMAS TERM, 1927

House Report: no doubt he is very aggravating… He should know by now that I don't care to find him boiling heaven-knows-what witches' brew by the aid of two guttering candles on a windowsill.

Alan contested that his only disappointment was that the experiment was halted before the master got to see the result. But the report went on:

House Report: he is the kind of boy who is bound to be rather a problem in any school or community, being in some respects definitely anti-social.

English: I can forgive his writing, though it is the worst I have ever seen, and I try to view tolerantly his unswerving inexactitude and slipshod, dirty work... but I cannot forgive the stupidity of his attitude towards sane discussion on the New Testament.

Latin: he ought not to be in this form... He is ludicrously behind.

This image of Alan as scruffy, disorganized and difficult to control was to follow him throughout his life. But in terms of achievement, at least, all was about to change.

BONZO

Alan did pass his Latin exam but Mr Bensly refused to pay up. Alan later got him back, publishing an equation in a school paper that mocked the master's infamous beating stick **"Bonzo"**, which was in fact a sort of wooden clothes brush.

Best Friend Forever

With the advent of sixth form, Alan's fortunes both in and out of class began to improve. Although initially held back for a term, he was allowed to take maths with the sixth formers, under the guidance of a young priest called Donald Eperson. Though he admitted Alan needed work, Eperson also saw in him the seeds of real genius, encouraging him to aim high. "He thinks very rapidly and is apt to be 'brilliant'," Eperson wrote in an early report. "He is seldom defeated by a problem, but his methods are often crude, cumbersome and untidy. But thoroughness and polish will no doubt come in time." And his new tutor wasn't the only ally Alan found. In Eperson's class Alan also discovered a kindred spirit, and his first ever best friend.

Christopher Morcom

Christopher Morcom was in the year above Alan, but their friendship was instant, bonding during a discussion on the orbit of planets. They found they shared a love of science and maths, and spent as much time as they could together, often working in the library after class. Then, in the holidays they wrote to each other – usually about things like physics, chemistry and astronomy. Most importantly, Christopher's ability and dedication inspired Alan. It was inevitable then that, faced with Christopher's imminent departure to university, Alan should want to go too.

Despite only being seventeen at the time, Alan went to Cambridge with Christopher to try for a maths scholarship – a week he described as "the best in my life". That happiness was short-lived, however. In December 1929, the results were published in the *Times*. While Christopher passed the exam with flying colours and was offered a scholarship to Trinity, Alan failed and had to face losing his friend for at least a year.

But worse was to come.

Goodbye to Morcom

At 2:45 a.m. on the night of the 6 February 1930, Alan had woken up and gone to the window, as he often did, to look at the stars through his telescope. That night though, the setting moon had seemed to him somewhat sorrowful, symbolizing a farewell to his friend: "Goodbye to Morcom". What Alan didn't know was that, at exactly the same time, this very friend was being rushed to hospital.

Christopher had contracted bovine tuberculosis as a child (TB) – again from infected cows' milk – and was weak as a result, and prone to illness. After two operations, and several days of hope and prayer, Christopher died in hospital. Alan was devastated, admitting he doubted he would ever find another friend like him. In a letter to his mother, he wrote:

"IT NEVER SEEMED TO HAVE OCCURRED TO ME TO MAKE OTHER FRIENDS BESIDES MORCOM: HE MADE EVERYONE ELSE SEEM SO ORDINARY."

Alan did make more friends, of course, including Victor Beuttell – another misfit who shared an interest in codes. But Christopher was far from forgotten, and Alan was more determined than ever to make him proud.

"I KNOW I MUST PUT AS MUCH ENERGY IF NOT AS MUCH INTEREST INTO MY WORK AS IF HE WERE ALIVE, BECAUSE THAT IS WHAT HE WOULD LIKE ME TO DO,"

he wrote to Mrs Morcom. And Alan kept his word.

The once despaired-of schoolboy gained a distinction in his final exams at Sherborne. He also won the "Morcom Prize" for science, set up in Christopher's name, not once but twice. And, best of all, he sat the Cambridge entrance exam a second time, and, though he failed to get a scholarship to Trinity, Alan was offered a place at King's. While he was initially disappointed, this second place was a stroke of luck that was to change the course of Alan's life, for King's was not only the home of many maths greats but also of secret government codebreakers.

Before that, though, there was just the small matter of "inventing" the computer.

GOAT MILK

Alan went on to become good friends with Christopher's mother, Mrs Morcom, and visited her at home, where she kept goats, a fact that seemed to astound many people. But it had been for a good reason: to ensure Christopher had a safe supply of milk (goats didn't carry the same dangerous diseases as cows).

CAMBRIDGE AND THE COMPUTER

A Natural Academic

In contrast to the invasive and rigid life at Sherborne, Cambridge – and King's in particular – was a natural and happy home for Alan. He made friends there and, though none of them could replace Christopher, many were to remain close to him for life. Importantly, he was allowed privacy, no longer having to share space with any other boys. So, with his untidiness largely ignored, he could get on with the business of being Alan, which he did with enthusiasm and style.

Although his first year was a bit of a disappointment academically (he only scraped through, having had rather too much fun, as many students often do), he soon got into the pace of things and began to shine, as well as make quite a name for himself, even arguing several times in lectures with the famous philosopher, Ludwig Wittgenstein.

After three years of hard work, Alan gained a first-class honours degree in maths and was made a "fellow" – the first in his year – meaning he could stay on to study for another year and be paid for it. However, university wasn't all about studying.

A CLOSED DOOR

Rooms at King's had two doors, an inner and an outer door. If a student had closed his outer door, it was known as "sporting the oak" and meant he was not to be disturbed. Alan took full advantage of this.

WITTGENSTEIN

Ludwig Wittgenstein was a German philosopher, fascinated with logic and mathematics, as well as language. He died in 1951.

Extra-Curricular Activities

Having missed out on music as a boy, Alan took up the violin, although he wasn't particularly good at it. He also started rowing, which he *was* rather good at, despite having shown little aptitude for sport at Sherborne at all. This was seen as unusual at the time – students were either athletes or they were "aesthetes" (meaning they cared only for art and beauty). But Alan was never one to conform to the rules.

This "joining in" also goes against the view many historians have conjured up of Alan as an unsociable loner. In fact he enjoyed debate, at least with his male colleagues at King's.

But these were, of course, just pastimes. It was in the classroom, and alone in his study, that Alan truly excelled, using his unique outlook to tackle an age-old question, with astounding results.

ASPERGER'S SYNDROME

Many people now believe that Alan had a condition called Asperger's syndrome, which is a form of Autism. Though each person living with Asperger's has a different experience, some argue that this would explain certain characteristics Alan exhibited, such as his general untidiness and lack of social skills.

PORGY

Having never been given a teddy bear when he was a child, he wrote to his parents to ask for one for Christmas. In 1934, "Porgy" arrived and stayed at his side for life. Alan even practised his lectures in front of Porgy. Porgy can be seen on display now at Bletchley Park, where Alan worked during World War Two.

Porgy Bear

Mechanical Maths

In 1920, a maths professor called David Hilbert had claimed that there should be "no knowable unknowns" in maths. In other words, every maths problem should be provable if you only follow the rules. Encouraged by his tutor, Max Newman (a man who was to inspire him and work alongside him throughout his career), Alan decided to try to prove what Hilbert had said himself.

In one of his lectures, Newman had talked about

"systematic procedures" in maths. By that he meant the rules we use to solve each particular maths problem, like subtracting or dividing or adding up. Key to these processes was that, once you knew the rules, you could do any calculation without any further knowledge – just using a pen and paper. In other words, processes so simple and structured that a machine could do them. What, Alan thought, if you could truly "mechanize" the process of maths? If you could make machines that would do the maths for you? To us, that might seem an obvious question with an even more obvious answer: yes. But back then it seemed wildly unusual, although it wasn't an entirely new concept.

From Analytical Engine to Universal Machine

In the 1800s, a man called Charles Babbage had invented his "Analytical Engine" – a sort of mechanical calculator. But, though it had been revolutionary in its time, the machine had never actually been finished. And so, the word "computer" continued to mean a human – a man or a woman – doing calculations by hand. Alan's idea was to change all this. He wrote,

"IT IS POSSIBLE TO INVENT A SINGLE MACHINE WHICH CAN BE USED TO COMPUTE ANY COMPUTABLE SEQUENCE."

What he imagined wasn't just a simple calculator for adding up, but a machine – a bit like a typewriter – that could do anything a human computer could do, just by following a set of rules (or "program") fed into it by means of limitless tape. This tape would be "read" by a scanner and the answer "printed" on the same moving tape. To change the settings, you simply changed the instructions on the tape, just as we flick from Internet to games to email on our devices. And, crucially, all the instructions would be written in "binary".

Charles
Babbage

CHARLES BABBAGE

Charles was what is known as a polymath. This means he was good at a lot of things, including, for Charles, maths and engineering. Born in 1791, he was educated mainly at home because he was often ill.

Alan later declared that Babbage's Analytical Engine machine wasn't a very attractive idea, as it would have been very slow, even compared to Alan's invention, which was positively snail-like compared to our computers today.

How Binary Works

Binary is another way of writing numbers, but only using two numerals (1 and 0) instead of the ten that we usually use (which is called the decimal system). It works because we break down the bigger numbers into columns. For example, the number 137 works like this in decimal:

100s	10s	1s
1	3	7

So we have 1 x 100, plus 3 x 10, plus 7 x 1 = 137

In binary, each column represents the number 2 to the power of x, where x means "another number" and "to the power of" means multiplied by itself that many times. For example:

2 to the power of 3 is 2 x 2 x 2.
So 2 x 2 = 4.
Then 4 x 2 = 8

So you get:
2 to the power of 0 = 0
2 to the power of 1 = 2
2 to the power of 2 = 4
2 to the power of 3 = 8
2 to the power of 4 = 16
2 to the power of 5 = 32
2 to the power of 6 = 64
2 to the power of 7 = 128

Q: Can you work out what 2 to the power of 8 is?

So, in binary, the number 137 is represented like this:

128	64	32	16	8	4	2	1
1	0	0	0	1	0	0	1

Because $128 + 8 + 1 = 137$

Why not try some more for yourself. Can you work out how to represent the following numbers in binary?

74

128	64	32	16	8	4	2	1

103

128	64	32	16	8	4	2	1

25

128	64	32	16	8	4	2	1

And how about reversing the process? How would you write these binary numbers using the decimal system?

0	0	0	0	1	0	1	0

answer ....

0	0	1	0	1	1	1	1

answer ....

1	0	1	0	1	0	1	1

answer ....

(Answers on page 199)

The Universal Machine

··

This was the genius of Alan's machine. Because any instruction can be coded in binary, the machine would be all-purpose, or "universal". In other words, it would be what we think of today as a "computer".

It's hard for us, in the age of smartphones and laptops and Google, to understand quite how ground-breaking this idea was. The idea of a machine that could solve any problem was arguably as game-changing as the apple falling on Newton's head showing him that gravity existed, or the discovery that Earth was round, not flat. In other words, in their time, they all probably sounded as far-fetched to an ordinary person like you or me being told now that in a few years we'll all be flying around with jetpacks. What's possibly more astounding, even to us in the modern day, is that this incredible invention was really just a by-product of Alan trying to prove another mathematician wrong, which he did, showing that there would always be some arithmetical truths that cannot be proven by machine. In other words, by following the rules.

Alan started to write up his results as an article or "paper" for the *Journal of the London Mathematical Society*. It was called *On Computable Numbers* (which is rather uninspiring given its fascinating content). Unfortunately for Alan, though, someone else had pipped him to the post, at least on the issue of Hilbert.

MODERN COMPUTERS

All computers today work on exactly the same principle as Alan's Universal Machine – binary code.

Scooped

Before Alan could send his paper off, another paper landed on the desk of his mentor, Max Newman. This one was written by an

American called Alonzo Church, and, not only had Church managed to prove the same thing as Alan, but his theory had already been published – this was what's known as a "scoop". Aside from getting something wrong, this is absolutely the worst thing that can happen to an academic, making years of work useless, and sending them scuttling back to their studies to find other apparently unsolvable problems to try their luck on. Fortunately for Alan, though, Newman was not at all disheartened.

Far from being despondent about the results, Newman realized that, while the end claim was the same, Alan's means to that end went far beyond Church's paper. In inventing the Universal Machine, Alan had laid the foundations for a whole new kind of science – computing. So Newman wrote to the London Mathematical Society asking them to publish Alan's paper anyway, which they did. On top of that, he wrote to Church himself, asking if he might offer Alan a place at Princeton University, where he was teaching.

Church agreed, and so, at the age of twenty-four, Alan was to leave his beloved Cambridge for America.

PIPPED TO THE POST

This wasn't the first time Alan had been beaten to a reveal. At school he had painstakingly proven a complicated maths theory only to be told someone else had done it years before. His version though, was simpler, and therefore, according to him, far better.

And it happened again at Cambridge when he proved the "central limit theorem". But, he and his tutors were unaware that this had already been proven in 1922 by Finnish mathematician, Jarl Waldemar Lindeberg.

Jarl Waldemar Lindberg.

Princeton and the PhD

Just like his journey to Sherborne ten years before, Alan's passage to America was not an easy one.

There were no commercial flights back then, and so Alan had to travel by sea, aboard the Cunard White Star Line's *Berengaria*, named after Richard I's wife, Queen Berengaria of Navarre. The luxury liner was enormous, housing more than 1,000 crew and 4,000 passengers, and quite glamourous. It had a Ritz-Carlton restaurant, promenade decks, shops, a tea garden and a ballroom. Alan's experience, unfortunately, was far from the stuff of dreams.

He had bought the cheapest possible ticket, known as "steerage", meaning he had a cramped cabin and spent an awful lot of time squashed in with fellow fourth-class passengers, an experience which probably reminded him of the worst of school. On top of that, many of the other people on board were American (of course), and Alan took an instant dislike to them, especially the way they seemed to say "aha" a lot during conversation. Ashore in New York, things weren't much better, with Alan complaining about having to queue at immigration for hours among screaming children, and then being "swindled" by a New York taxi driver for what he saw as a steep fare (it wasn't; Alan was just unused to paying for taxis). But, the journey over, he was at last in America, and about to further his career with the highest academic qualification possible: a PhD, giving him the title "Doctor".

Gaining a doctorate is notoriously difficult, and Alan certainly found it so, complaining in letters home that he was making little progress and having to constantly rewrite his ideas. This, though, seems to have been measured by Alan's exacting standards. In fact, he passed in just eighteen months – most candidates take at least three years – and was offered a fellowship position, meaning he could carry on his research alongside teaching. Instead, in 1938, he opted to return to Cambridge and to his fellowship there. Alan, it seemed, had other plans.

And so, too, did the Germans.

SURRENDER

RMS *Berengaria* was originally a German vessel called SS *Imperator*, but was surrendered to America after World War One.

Cunard White Star Line's 'Berengaria'

The Old Boys' Network

It was 1938, and with Hitler on the rise and war in Europe on the horizon, everyone's lives were changing. The horrors of *Kristallnacht* (or the

Night of Broken Glass) – when the Nazis smashed Jewish homes, schools and synagogues, and incarcerated 30,000 Jewish men in concentration camps – saw the arrival in Britain of a small number of Jewish refugees. Determined to do his bit to help, and following the example of a friend from King's called Fred Clayton, Alan cycled to the refugee camp in Harwich. There he met Robert Augenfeld (known as Bob), a boy who was keen to continue his studies in science, something close to Alan's heart. Alan and Fred helped Bob and his friend, Karl, find foster homes and school places in Lancashire.

But Alan was about to play a much bigger role in the war. Because, as the government began to assemble troops to outfight the Germans, it also needed to assemble great minds to outwit them.

During World War One, the ability to break German naval codes had been key and the effort had been run largely by a group of men from Alan's old Cambridge college, King's. Knowing that this need was imminent again, the powers-that-be began to draw up a list of brilliant minds who might be good at that sort of thing. As well as chess players, and others clever at solving puzzles, they of course looked to King's and its mathematicians, putting down the names of eleven fellows and eight graduates. Among the fellows listed was Alan Turing.

MANCHESTER UNIVERSITY

Bob did well at school and got a place studying chemistry at Manchester University, where Alan was later to work.

A Double Life

As war approached, Alan had begun giving his first lectures at King's, although he complained to his mother that only fourteen people had shown up, and that he expected even that to drop off as the year progressed. Clearly, his genius had yet to emerge, at least to undergraduates. But disappointing attendance was rather a side matter as, alongside his academic responsibilities, Alan was being kept busy on hush-hush government business.

Along with the other recruits, Alan was being sent on secret courses in London to learn about the "Enigma" machine. Looking like an overcomplicated typewriter, this contraption was used by German forces to "encrypt" messages before they were sent out in Morse code, making it all but impossible for anyone to read them. Alan, though, had already shown himself to be a natural at codes and ciphers, working on his own encryption machine whilst at Princeton, which he had even suggested selling to the government in a letter to his mother. In light of that, he may well have welcomed the difficult work on the Enigma.

Whatever the case, this small, devious machine was to take over his life for the foreseeable future. And for that, all of us should be grateful, for Alan's singular genius not only cracked the machine, but saved millions of lives in the process.

SECRET CIPHERS

The Caesar Shift

Before we get back to Alan and his work on the elusive Enigma, it's worth understanding a bit about how codes, ciphers and the Enigma machine itself work.

A "code" is when whole words are replaced. A "cipher" is when each individual letter is replaced or rearranged, making it much harder to solve. Ciphers have been used for centuries to pass messages in secret, especially in times of war. The Roman leader Caesar used a method now called the "Caesar shift". This replaced each letter of the alphabet with a different one, by shunting the letters along. For example:

A	B	C	D	E	F	G	H	I	J	K	L	M	N	O	P	Q	R	S	T	U	V	W	X	Y	Z
C	D	E	F	G	H	I	J	K	L	M	N	O	P	Q	R	S	T	U	V	W	X	Y	Z	A	B

This has a Caesar shift of two, because the

cipher letters are shunted along by two places. This rule is known as the "key". To encrypt a message, you replace the "plain text" letters with the "cipher text" ones below. So, with the key "Caesar shift of two":

SEND TROOPS QUICKLY

changes to

UGPF VTQQRU SWKEMNA

At first glance this looks like gobbledegook, but once you know the key it's actually really easy to work out. Using the same Caesar shift, try these messages for size (you can then find the answers on page 199):

C	N	C	P		V	W	T	K	P	I		C	V	G		C	P		C	R	R	N	G		C		F	C	A

C	N	C	P		J	C	F		C		D	G	C	T		E	C	N	N	G	F		R	Q	T	I	A

Even if you don't know the key, it's not impossible to solve. Can you see how the letter C appears a lot in the encrypted messages? That's because certain letters are used in words more often than others (which is why A is worth a lot less than Q in Scrabble). In this case, the letter C corresponds to A, which we know is used a lot in English. This is called "frequency" or a "crib" and is one of the most important tools in cipher-breaking.

ANCIENT GREECE

In 499 BCE, the ancient Greek tyrant, Histiaeus, shaved the head of his most trusted slave, tattooed a message on his head, waited for his hair to grow back, then sent him to his son-in-law, Aristagoras, with the instruction to shave him. The message told Aristagoras to revolt against the Persians, which he did.

Monoalphabetic Ciphers

To make messages harder to break, cryptologists looked for better ways to encrypt messages. One way was to randomize letters completely instead of just shifting them along. For example:

A	B	C	D	E	F	G	H	I	J	K	L	M	N	O	P	Q	R	S	T	U	V	W	X	Y	Z
T	F	K	Z	C	J	Q	O	B	A	Y	M	P	N	U	W	D	L	G	E	X	H	V	S	I	R

This cipher is still fairly easy to break using the frequency method though, as the letter T will appear a lot in the cipher text, replacing A. E will also appear frequently, replacing T (as "the" is a common word in English). Both this and the Caesar shift are known as "monoalphabetic" ciphers, because they swap the alphabet once. So, it makes sense that swapping letters more than once will make the cipher harder to crack.

Polyalphabetic Ciphers

This next step is called a "polyalphabetic" cipher. This swaps the alphabet over not once but often several times, so that each letter of the plain-text cipher might be encrypted differently each time. The trickiest of all of these was called the Vigenère square, which had twenty-six columns and twenty-six rows, each with a Caesar shift of one.

	A	B	C	D	E	F	G	H	I	J	K	L	M	N	O	P	Q	R	S	T	U	V	W	X	Y	Z
A	A	B	C	D	E	F	G	H	I	J	K	L	M	N	O	P	Q	R	S	T	U	V	W	X	Y	Z
B	B	C	D	E	F	G	H	I	J	K	L	M	N	O	P	Q	R	S	T	U	V	W	X	Y	Z	A
C	C	D	E	F	G	H	I	J	K	L	M	N	O	P	Q	R	S	T	U	V	W	X	Y	Z	A	B
D	D	E	F	G	H	I	J	K	L	M	N	O	P	Q	R	S	T	U	V	W	X	Y	Z	A	B	C
E	E	F	G	H	I	J	K	L	M	N	O	P	Q	R	S	T	U	V	W	X	Y	Z	A	B	C	D
F	F	G	H	I	J	K	L	M	N	O	P	Q	R	S	T	U	V	W	X	Y	Z	A	B	C	D	E
G	G	H	I	J	K	L	M	N	O	P	Q	R	S	T	U	V	W	X	Y	Z	A	B	C	D	E	F
H	H	I	J	K	L	M	N	O	P	Q	R	S	T	U	V	W	X	Y	Z	A	B	C	D	E	F	G
I	I	J	K	L	M	N	O	P	Q	R	S	T	U	V	W	X	Y	Z	A	B	C	D	E	F	G	H
J	J	K	L	M	N	O	P	Q	R	S	T	U	V	W	X	Y	Z	A	B	C	D	E	F	G	H	I
K	K	L	M	N	O	P	Q	R	S	T	U	V	W	X	Y	Z	A	B	C	D	E	F	G	H	I	J
L	L	M	N	O	P	Q	R	S	T	U	V	W	X	Y	Z	A	B	C	D	E	F	G	H	I	J	K
M	M	N	O	P	Q	R	S	T	U	V	W	X	Y	Z	A	B	C	D	E	F	G	H	I	J	K	L
N	N	O	P	Q	R	S	T	U	V	W	X	Y	Z	A	B	C	D	E	F	G	H	I	J	K	L	M
O	O	P	Q	R	S	T	U	V	W	X	Y	Z	A	B	C	D	E	F	G	H	I	J	K	L	M	N
P	P	Q	R	S	T	U	V	W	X	Y	Z	A	B	C	D	E	F	G	H	I	J	K	L	M	N	O
Q	Q	R	S	T	U	V	W	X	Y	Z	A	B	C	D	E	F	G	H	I	J	K	L	M	N	O	P
R	R	S	T	U	V	W	X	Y	Z	A	B	C	D	E	F	G	H	I	J	K	L	M	N	O	P	Q
S	S	T	U	V	W	X	Y	Z	A	B	C	D	E	F	G	H	I	J	K	L	M	N	O	P	Q	R
T	T	U	V	W	X	Y	Z	A	B	C	D	E	F	G	H	I	J	K	L	M	N	O	P	Q	R	S
U	U	V	W	X	Y	Z	A	B	C	D	E	F	G	H	I	J	K	L	M	N	O	P	Q	R	S	T
V	V	W	X	Y	Z	A	B	C	D	E	F	G	H	I	J	K	L	M	N	O	P	Q	R	S	T	U
W	W	X	Y	Z	A	B	C	D	E	F	G	H	I	J	K	L	M	N	O	P	Q	R	S	T	U	V
X	X	Y	Z	A	B	C	D	E	F	G	H	I	J	K	L	M	N	O	P	Q	R	S	T	U	V	W
Y	Y	Z	A	B	C	D	E	F	G	H	I	J	K	L	M	N	O	P	Q	R	S	T	U	V	W	X
Z	Z	A	B	C	D	E	F	G	H	I	J	K	L	M	N	O	P	Q	R	S	T	U	V	W	X	Y

This is how it worked:

Firstly, it needed a plain-text message, such as, ATTACK TONIGHT. Then it needed a key, such as, TURING. The key would be written out repeatedly above the plain-text message, like this:

T	U	R	I	N	G	T	U	R	I	N	G	T
A	T	T	A	C	K	T	O	N	I	G	H	T

The key told the user which row to use to encrypt each letter. So here, the letter A at the beginning of the message must be encrypted using the horizontal row beginning T. The cryptographer would use the vertical row beginning A and run down to find where it met the horizontal row beginning T, to find the letter A. Then the letter T would be encrypted using the row beginning U. See if you can finish encrypting the message below.

T	U	R	I	N	G	T	U	R	I	N	G	T
A	T	T	A	C	K	T	O	N	I	G	H	T
T												

But, even though the alphabet was swapped more than once, a letter could still be encrypted the same way more than once, especially if it was a short key.

If you look at the example above, the key "TURING" limits the different potential swaps for each letter to six, because it's six letters long. Even here, the letter T is twice coded using the row beginning T, meaning it will end up the same. So, the longer the key, the better. But even this didn't stop Charles Babbage (remember him?) breaking the cipher. So, by the turn of the twentieth century, cryptographers began to look elsewhere for a new "unbreakable" method. One that used a really long, randomized key. And preferably one that was faster to use than the complicated paper and pen method.

Enter Arthur Scherbius and the Enigma machine.

Arthur Scherbius

The Enigma Machine

Born in Frankfurt in 1878, Arthur Scherbius studied electrical engineering and went on to patent all sorts of incredible inventions including an electric pillow. The one that has gone down in history, however, is the Enigma.

Named for the Greek word for "riddle", the contraption was originally intended as a commercial machine, to help banks encrypt important financial information. Sales were disappointing, but Scherbius was undeterred, refining the machine to make it smaller and more portable, convinced it would eventually find its market.

He was right. While businesses couldn't see the attraction (and nor could the British authorities, who short-sightedly turned down a machine), the German military, swelling in power and preparing for action, knew they had found the ideal way to keep their important messages from reaching the wrong people.

SCHERBIUS

Scherbius copied the design of the Enigma machine from two Dutch naval officers, who had tried to patent it themselves and failed.

But, he never got to enjoy fame, or even see the reach of his machine at its peak: he died in a horse-carriage accident in 1929.

How the Enigma Works

At first glance, the Enigma looked simple. Every time a plain-text letter was hit on the typewriter keyboard, a different encrypted letter lit up on the lamp board above it. The series of illuminated letters formed the cipher text. This was then written down and given to a radio operator, who coded it into Morse and sent that across the airwaves. At the other end, on receiving the Morse code, another radio operator would translate the Morse into cipher text, input that into an Enigma machine and, as long as the machines were set up in exactly the same way, out would come the plain-text message.

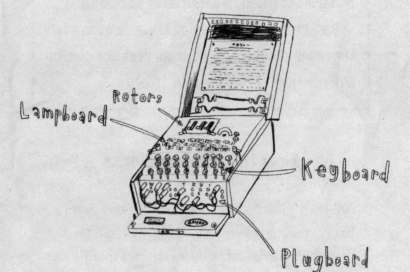

Enigma machine

Lampboard

Rotors

Keyboard

Plugboard

MORSE CODE

Morse code translates the alphabet into a series of dots and dashes, or long sounds and short sounds. This means words can be sent, letter by letter, in a series of long and short beeps.

Intercepting the Morse code messages was easy enough – hundred of "Y stations" around the world were "listening in" and noting down every single transmission. These transcripts were then sent to British code headquarters, Bletchley Park, via teleprinter or underwater cable where they were translated back into letters. But, of course, these transcripts appeared as nonsense, and working out what they really meant was no picnic.

The reason lay in the horribly complicated system of wheels and cables and reflectors inside the Enigma machine, which could change a letter several times, in literally millions of ways, between the initial keyboard stroke and the lamp being illuminated. This is how it did it:

1. Each Enigma had three different rotors or "wheels", each marked up with the twenty-six letters of the alphabet. These were loaded on to the rod in a particular order, and turned to their start position, for example EXM. This was called the "wheel setting" and "day key", and a cryptologist would need to know both to be able to read any message sent through the machine. At first there were three wheels, giving 17,576 possible wheel settings. But the Germans soon upped that so that the three wheels in use each day were chosen out of an available five, increasing the possible settings even further. But it didn't end there.

2. Each time a key was pressed, one of the wheels would click round, altering the setting. Then, after a certain number of clicks, according to a notch cut into the side of the wheel, the first wheel would force the second wheel to click on as well, changing the setting further. And on and on with each wheel clicking round and round, changing the key at every keyboard stroke.

3. Not only that, but each of the wheels had different internal wiring that could be altered slightly by use of a spring-loaded ring. This was called the "ring setting" and any cryptologist would need to know that as well.

4. And, as if that wasn't complicated enough, once the letter had passed through the wheel system, changing three times along the way, it hit a "reflector" that sent it back through the three wheels on a different route, changing again at every wheel. And there was more to come.

5. At the front of the Enigma machine was a series of sockets and jacks called the "plugboard". Each socket was marked up with a letter of the alphabet, allowing the operator to connect two letters and effectively swap them over before they even got as far as the wheels. There were six different jacks in use for each "plugboard setting", though, again, the Germans soon upped this to ten.

All in all, this took the number of possible Enigma settings up to 159 million million million, each of which might have to be checked before a message could be decrypted.

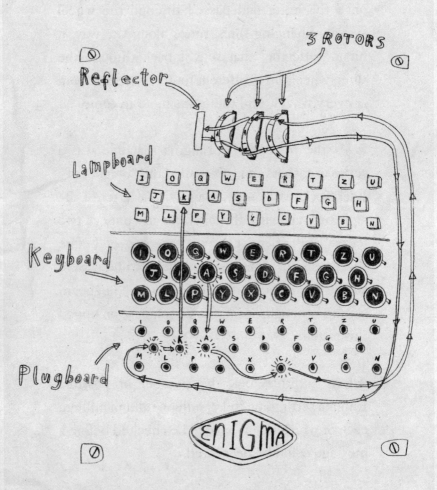

Key Complications

• •

And it got worse again.

The initial settings for the wheels and plugboard were recorded in a codebook and given to every Enigma operator. They might read something like this:

Plugboard: G/K – M/U – K/S – B/T – S/W – N/L
Wheel order: 2-3-1
Wheel settings: V-K-P

But the initial wheel settings, or "day key", were only used for one thing: to set another key. Before each message was sent, the day key was used to transmit a new three-letter wheel setting, called the "message key", which was chosen at random by the operator. The wheels would then be changed to the new starting positions and the actual message could finally be encrypted and sent.

In turn, having received the message key via Morse code, and deciphered it on the Enigma machine at the other end, that operator would then switch the wheels to their new starting positions before typing in the next encrypted Morse message. If everything had been done "by the book", out would come a plain-text instruction in perfect German.

Here, then, was the polyalphabetic cipher to end all polyalphabetic ciphers. Even using a replica Enigma machine, without access to the secret German codebooks that listed each day's Enigma settings for the month (before the book was swapped to a new codebook), each setting would have to be checked by hand. And checking that many settings by hand would take longer than the time elapsed since the universe had begun. Britain needed a better way of doing it. It needed to break Enigma. And to do that, it needed the brilliant minds at Bletchley, and specifically that of Alan Turing.

AN EASIER WAY?

Of course, getting hold of the codebooks would have been a quick and easy way to break the

Enigma, but the Germans were far too clever for that, at least at the beginning.

Enigma code books

BLETCHLEY AND THE BOMBE

Reporting to Bletchley

On 1 September 1939, Hitler finally did what he'd been threatening and invaded Poland. Outraged (though unsurprised), Britain gave Germany a deadline of 11 a.m. on 3 September to withdraw its troops, but Germany didn't respond. And so, at 11.15 that morning, Prime Minister Neville Chamberlain announced that Britain was at war. Within minutes, well-laid plans were put into action and Alan was ordered to leave his job in Cambridge. The following day, with no idea when – or even if – he might be going back, he took a train to Buckinghamshire, left his luggage at his lodgings or "billet" – the Crown pub – and reported for duty at the Government Code & Cipher School (GC&CS) headquarters in Bletchley Park.

Bletchley Park

Bletchley Park was a smallish country house with gardens and outbuildings, soon to be joined by a number of "huts" where Alan would eventually work, running Hut 8. For a stately home it was all rather underwhelming, and Bletchley itself wasn't much better. It was a small sort of town – often complained about by the workers at GC&CS because there was so little to do and so little to see. But that was part of the point. Being a small, nondescript sort of town, Bletchley was unlikely to be the target of German bombs.

It was also usefully positioned – just under fifty miles from London, so close enough to be accessible in a couple of hours, as well as being exactly between Oxford and Cambridge, the two top recruiting grounds for codebreakers, or "men of the professor type", as Bletchley deputy head, Commander Alastair Denniston, called them. The other "men of the professor type" included Hugh Alexander, the British chess champion and Stuart Milner-Barry, the *Times* chess correspondent, as well as another Cambridge mathematician, Gordon Welchman. Together with Alan, they were sent to the "Cottage" (actually an old stable block) and assigned the job of cracking Enigma.

CRYPTIC CROSSWORD CHALLENGE

In a bid to recruit more puzzle-solving minds that might be good for deciphering work, GC&CS placed an announcement in the *Daily Telegraph*. It said that if anyone could solve that day's "cryptic" crossword in less than twelve minutes they were to get in touch. Of course, the ad was careful not to mention Bletchley or the work GC&CS had in mind.

Twenty-five people replied and were asked to come to a special test in Fleet Street in London. There, they were given another crossword to complete. Five managed to do it in the allotted time, and another one had only one clue left. All six were recruited to Bletchley's code-breaking huts.

CLUES AND PATTERNS

Cryptic crosswords use many of the same ideas as codes, so if you can crack one, you might be able to crack the other.

Each crossword designer or "setter" uses their own method and often repeats it. The trick is to look for clues and patterns.

The Need for Secrecy

The operation of GC&CS relied on utmost secrecy. Alan, like all his colleagues, had to sign the Official Secrets Act, promising not to talk to anyone about what he was doing, meaning he couldn't say a word to his family or friends about his new job. Even within Bletchley, what each person did was kept on the hush-hush, to the point that two sisters who both worked there had no idea what the other was doing.

Another obstacle that had to be overcome was how to explain their sudden presence to the locals, especially because they weren't in uniform. Were they conscientious objectors perhaps, opposed to the war? In the summer of 1938, there had been a "rehearsal", with a group of codebreakers visiting the site under the guise of "Captain Ridley's Shooting Party" (in reality, Captain Ridley was an M16 naval officer). If asked, they could just tell curious locals they were off to shoot game birds. But with the number of workers set to rise to the thousands, that excuse wouldn't work, and so staff were told to claim they were "part of the aerial defence of London". In the long term, this secrecy cost Alan and many other Bletchley workers greatly, as their heroic deeds would go unrecognized for decades. They would have to pretend they had done nothing of note at all during the war, which was frowned upon terribly. Right now, though, the war was just beginning, and secrecy was essential. As was the need for speed.

The Polish Head Start

Breaking Enigma wasn't just a matter of British pride, or one in the eye for Hitler; it had a real purpose. Each message was of vital importance to Germany, giving details of troop movements and planned attacks. If the British could read the messages in time, they could avoid hits and plan their own counter-attacks, saving lives as well as making sure essential fuel and food got across to British shores. But it was "in time" that was key. How to get from "all the seconds in the universe" needed to go through the possible

Enigma settings to a matter of days, or preferably hours? Luckily, Alan and the rest of his Bletchley colleagues had got a bit of a head start, with the help of some European friends.

Years previously, the British military had written off Enigma as entirely unsolvable, insisting it would be foolish wasting time and money trying to break it. Over on the Continent though, one country couldn't afford to be so dismissive. Poland neighboured Germany and, with Hitler gaining power and threatening invasion, the Poles had no choice but to give breaking Enigma a try.

Marian Rejewski

The name of Marian Rejewski is still little-known today outside Poland, but he was key to the story of World War Two, and to Alan's own story. Thanks to some photographs of Enigma settings taken by a German spy, Hans-Thilo Schmidt, who was secretly working for the French, Rejewski managed to crack certain elements of the machine. Fast forward to 1939, just weeks before war broke out, and Bletchley's deputy head, Commander Denniston, and Dilly Knox, the senior cryptographer, were sent to a secret meeting in some woods near Warsaw.

Here the Poles handed over everything they had worked out about Enigma so far. This meant that, by the time Alan arrived at Bletchley, GC&CS already knew the internal wiring of the three wheels, as well the wiring of another crucial part of the device called the "entry board". On top of that, the Poles had discovered that the Germans had some "rules" about using the Enigma:

1. The wheels weren't allowed to be in the same position for more than two days in a row. This meant some settings could be ruled out.

2. The plugboard didn't allow for next-door letters to be swapped. So, M could not be swapped with L or N for example, which also cut a number of settings out.

3. Once the Germans set the "day key", they would use it to send the same "message key" twice over.

All of these had helped the Poles crack plenty of messages. But with the volume of messages or "traffic" on the increase, the key was being changed daily instead of every few months. The number of casualties was on the rise, and the threat of German cipher security was getting tighter, so Alan and others needed another leap forward. They needed a "crib".

Clever Cribbing

Reading and rereading old decrypted messages, Alan realized that some words appeared again and again. For example, the first message of the day was often a weather report, so the German word for weather – WETTER – was often used. This was called a "crib", which means cheat. By comparing this crib to the cipher text, they could feasibly work out the setting. Key to this was another flaw in the way Enigma worked.

Enigma had been designed so that it would never encrypt a letter as itself. So W would never appear as W, or E as E, or T as T, and so on. This meant it was easier to find the exact location of the crib within the cipher text. So the cryptologists would slide suspected cribs along the cipher text looking for a position where no letters matched. Any matches were called "crashes". The longer the crib was, the more likely it was to crash, so the easier it was to find the right position.

Alan's team also worked out that, even though they weren't supposed to, Enigma operators often took shortcuts when thinking up their message keys. Sometimes they'd just pick three letters that were next to each other on the keyboard. Sometimes they'd use the initials of their girlfriend, or the first three letters of their own name, such as, CIL. These mistakes, which cost the Germans dear, were nicknamed "cillies" because of that oft-repeated key from one lazy operator.

So, with a good crib, and a lot of time and patience, it was possible to fiddle with an Enigma's wheels and plugboard until the message was decoded. But time was in short supply. Alan needed a faster way of checking potential settings. And that was Alan's second stroke of genius. If messages were being encrypted by machine, didn't it follow that a machine would be the best thing to decrypt them?

HITLER'S DOWNFALL

Another brilliant crib was "HEIL HITLER" which appeared at the end of many messages. It became a joke that Hitler's own vanity had been his downfall.

The Bombe

The Poles had certainly seen the importance of mechanizing the decryption process – they'd built a machine called a "bomba". While this was named after the ice cream, not the explosive device, its effect on Enigma encryption had certainly been devastating. But the Polish technology was rendered useless as soon as the Germans had stopped using their repeated message code. What Alan had in mind wouldn't be susceptible to such changes. It would rely on cribs not a repeat key, it would be adaptable, and above all, it would be quick.

Alan's "Bombe" (named in honour of its Polish predecessor) was effectively a lot of Enigma machines wired together. The design used a series of drums, each one corresponding to a single Enigma wheel. The machine would then spin though all the settings at superhuman speed to see if it could find one that would change the letters in the crib into the letters in the cipher text. Each time the machine found a potential match it would come to a stop, with the three-letter key showing on its indicator drums. The operator would then use an Enigma machine to check this, along with its guess at the plugboard setting that showed on a panel at the side. If plain text came out, the match had been made, and hundreds more messages sent using the same key could be decrypted. If not, then it was back to the Bombe.

The Bombe

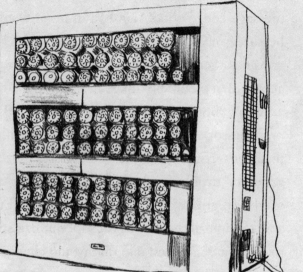

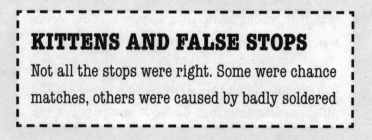

KITTENS AND FALSE STOPS

Not all the stops were right. Some were chance matches, others were caused by badly soldered

connections. These were called "false stops".
Stops were also called "kittening" because of
the strange sound the machine made.

Victory

With the help of a brilliant engineer called Doc
Keen, Alan's first bombe arrived at Bletchley
in March 1940. It had cost £6,500 to build (the
equivalent of a quarter of a million pounds today)
and was codenamed "Victory", although this
proved a misnomer, as the machine didn't quite
work as planned.

The problem was that, because the cribs were
too weak, the Bombe was finding too many stops.
In order to get better cribs they needed to have
more decrypted messages. But in order to get
more decrypted messages, they needed better
cribs – what's called a "catch-22" situation.

At that point, Alan's colleague, Gordon
Welchman, stepped in and devised something
called a "diagonal board" to help solve the

plugboard problem. Its cross-wiring meant the Bombe could move quicker and find fewer, better stops, cutting the checking time and meaning more messages could be decrypted quicker.

WHAT IS A CATCH-22?

Named after Joseph Heller's famous novel, a "catch-22" situation is one in which the answer to a question is prevented by the problem itself. For example: how can I look for my glasses when I've lost my glasses?

Lamb of God

A second Bombe, built according to Alan's design, and with Welchman's time-saving addition, was delivered to Bletchley in August. This one was called Agnus Dei, or "Lamb of God", who, according to the Bible, would "take away the sins of the world". While the name might have been over-egging it slightly, there was no denying the glorious truth: this version worked.

Agnes, as she was quickly known, was joined by another Bombe, and then another, until there was no room at Bletchley to house all the Bombes, and new ones had to be stationed on the outskirts of London. Together, they were helping decipher thousands of Enigma messages a month, giving Britain the edge on Germany, preventing Hitler's planned invasion of Britain and saving lives, though, significantly, not as many as they potentially could have.

BOMBES AWAY!

It was also important to have Bombes in more than one location in case Bletchley was hit and the machinery destroyed. The sound of the Bombes in action was like thousands of knitting needles, clacking away.

The Difficult Pay-off

· ·

What the British quickly realized was that, however much intelligence they gathered via the Bombes, they couldn't possibly act on all of it. Not because they didn't have the capacity, but because they would have given the game away if they had. Intelligence relied on staying one step ahead of Hitler, and that included not letting on that the Enigma had been broken, or they could be sure the Germans would change their methods immediately. If, for example, the Germans had sent a message saying they had U-boats stationed in a particular position, and British ships had immediately turned around to avoid them, it would have been highly suspicious. Instead, they had to use various methods to cover up their discoveries.

Sometimes, they would send out fake scout planes who could pretend to "find" the ships and thus legitimately send a signal to avoid them. At other times, though, they had to make the terrible decision to sacrifice their own troops, and even civilians.

The Coventry Blitz Conspiracy

The city of Coventry, in the industrial Midlands of Britain, had been attacked repeatedly in the first months of the war, but on 14 November 1940 came an assault like none the city had seen before. Some five hundred German bombers flew in, wave after wave, killing more than five hundred people and injuring nearly a thousand, and destroying or damaging more than 40,000 homes. The only reason the death toll was so low was that many people had taken to trekking out of the city at night to take shelter in nearby villages.

But could the toll have been lower still? A theory lingers to this day that the Coventry Blitz could have been prevented; that workers at Bletchley had decrypted messages telling them what was on the cards, but that Churchill was too scared to act in case the Germans worked out that Enigma had been compromised. Did he sacrifice the city to save the Enigma secret? Or had the Bombes actually failed, and not got to the messages in time or at all? The truth is we don't know and probably never will. We do know that Churchill had to pretend to be in the dark about other discoveries though.

In August 1941, Bletchley had deciphered a raft of German messages talking about the shooting of thousands of Jews. However, in Churchill's public message he only mentioned "scores of executions", careful to omit the word "Jew" altogether, for fear the Germans would work out how Britain knew such specifics.

All of this must have been difficult for those workers inside Bletchley's gates, knowing as much as they did and never being able to talk about it, especially if they had friends or relatives on board ships or living in cities about to be hit. But the fact was, there was a war on, and it was a bitter and bloody one.

CHURCHILL

Winston Churchill took over as prime minister in May 1940, after Neville Chamberlain resigned. Chamberlain died a few months later.

Winston Churchill

The War Outside

On the day Alan arrived at GC&CS, 17,000 children were also on the move, being evacuated to small towns and villages, including Bletchley, where they would be safer from bombing. Many protested and wanted to stay behind – it was scary, after all, to have to leave family and live (as Alan had) with strangers. The worst fears of the authorities were, however, well-founded. The Blitz began in September 1940, killing and injuring thousands of people. Whole streets

children evacuating at train platform

were destroyed, ruining lives and livelihoods. The nightly raids only eased off when Hitler began to focus on an invasion of Russia. Even with the intelligence supplied by Hut 6, which was working on messages from the German Air Force, over more than eight months of sustained attacks a total of 43,000 people were killed.

Inside Bletchley

· ·

Even Bletchley didn't escape in the end, one bomb dropping just thirty metres from Alan's billet at the Crown. But despite the threat and the stress of the work, normal life (or as normal as possible) rumbled on inside Bletchley's gates as best it could.

The place was practically a town in itself, with nearly 10,000 workers, most of them young, some of them straight from school. They were a varied bunch too, from the codebreakers themselves – whose numbers included not only the mathematicians and chess players, but a future novelist, Angus Wilson, and the one-day Home Secretary, Roy Jenkins – to the messengers and drivers who kept the place functioning. And they all needed a bit of downtime. That might be outings around the local area, games on the lawns at Bletchley, dances, or just a drink with friends – Hut 2 was known as the "beer hut" and served refreshments. There was also the chance to get a little rest and recuperation: Hut 5 was termed a "sunray parlour" or light-therapy room.

This wasn't for tanning, but rather to boost levels of Vitamin D (which we get from sunlight) for the workers who spent long hours in blacked-out rooms.

As well as being necessarily dark, Bletchley was also notoriously cold. There was little heating to speak of, and the blackout meant that choking fumes from leaky stoves got trapped in the rooms. In the end many workers, including Alan, took to knitting their own gloves.

It was, without doubt, an unusual place. One newcomer described it as "weird" and full of "weedy-looking men". Perhaps it was weird, but these weedy men were heroes, and none more so than "Prof", as he was now known.

LOOSE THREADS

Alan's gloves actually weren't too bad, but he didn't know how to sew the last bit and left threads of wool trailing from the ends of his fingers for ages until a colleague, Joan, helped him finish them off properly.

Fascinating Alan

Although he was only of the "professor type" and not an actual professor, Alan rather lived up to the image of being more concerned with work than appearance. His fear of blood meant he rarely shaved, and when he did it was with a rather useless electric shaver so that he had a permanent "five o'clock shadow". He had a high-pitched voice, and an apparently irritating laugh. He also had what sounded like a stammer, with Alan repeating the syllable "ah-ah-ah" at length mid-conversation. In fact, it was a deliberate trick Alan had devised to ensure no one could interrupt him.

He was still messy as well. Frank Birch, one of his superiors, wrote of him and a colleague called Twinn: "Like many brilliant men they are not practical. They are untidy, they lose things, they can't copy out right." While senior cryptographer, Dilly Knox, even went as far as complaining in a letter that, "He is very clever but quite irresponsible."

Alan was clever, if a little different. Take his

rickety old bicycle, the chain of which often came off. Instead of getting it fixed, he worked out precisely how many rotations it took before the chain messed up, and back-pedalled before it could happen. Perhaps he was trying to save money, but it also meant that no one else would "borrow" his bike.

On these bicycle rides in the summer months, he also took to wearing his gas mask. He wasn't worried about chemical attacks though; rather he suffered from terrible hay fever, and this stopped the pollen getting in – another canny invention. And his interesting habits didn't stop there.

Alan famously chained his tea mug to the radiator to stop anyone stealing it (tea mugs were in scarce supply in the war). According to many accounts he often slept in the Cottage or came to work still dressed in pyjamas. When he did wear trousers, they were invariably held up with string or a tie rather than belt or braces. No wonder Alan struggled with the military precision expected of members of the Home Guard which, like all Bletchley staff, he was expected to join.

Alan enjoyed aspects of this service, becoming

a brilliant shot, but the parades were a step too far for him, involving marching, neat uniform and polished boots. He refused to take part and faced a court martial for breaking military law. Alan, however, managed to escape scot-free on a technicality: when previously asked if he understood that, if he didn't follow orders, he'd be subject to military law, he'd answered "no".

The Silver Ingots

Perhaps the most extreme of Alan's eccentricities was his plan to protect his savings.

Fearing a destitute, or even invaded Britain post-war, Alan decided that a bank was not a safe place for his money. Instead, he used his savings to buy two silver bars or "ingots". Using an old pram, he wheeled these into the woods near Bletchley and buried them in different places, along with £200 in notes. He then wrote instructions on how to find them again, enciphered them, pushed them inside a decongestant inhaler and hid that under a bridge.

Unfortunately for Alan, the map and his memory failed him. Though he tried twice to dig them up after the war, with the help of a friend and a home-made metal detector, the silver ingots have never been found. (He was luckier with the pound notes, recovering these towards the end of the war, though, in typical Alan fashion, he'd dug them up before work, making him both late and muddy.)

ingots

STOCKPILING

Alan also suggested buying a suitcase full of razorblades, knowing these would be in short supply. Perhaps he thought he could sell them on street corners?

Alan and Joan

··

It might sound like all the work at Bletchley was done by men, but this was far from the case. The Bombes were operated by the Women's Royal Naval Service or "Wrens". By the end of the war there were thousands working on the machines, as well as waitresses in the canteen, secretaries and messengers. And they were as fascinating as the men, including famous actresses and even debutantes (rich, young celebrities). Alan tended to avoid all of them, even going as far as sneaking away if any of them approached him.

Unable to make "small talk", he preferred to converse only about the pressing matters at hand, or at least topics of importance like biology and maths. And these subjects were, for the most part, the preserve of men in those days. There was, however, at least one exception.

A former student of Gordon Welchman, Joan Clarke, was assigned to Alan's Hut 8. Joan and Alan had much in common – a love of nature, and of chess. They often played after the long night shift, at first using Joan's cardboard set and then,

Joan Clarke

later, a pottery set that they made together using clay from nearby pits, fired on the hob of the coal fire in Alan's room at the Crown. Of course, they were also both brilliant code-breakers. They became so close that Alan eventually proposed marriage and Joan accepted.

The engagement, however, was short-lived. Alan was gay and, in proposing to Joan, he'd only been trying to follow convention – in the 1940s, homosexuality was still a crime. But his honesty got the better of him and in the end he confessed to Joan. She, it seemed, didn't care, and was happy to remain engaged, which she saw as useful for both of them. But Alan couldn't bear the deceit and broke it off. Instead, they remained friends and colleagues, while Alan focused on his first – and perhaps only – real love: work.

WOMEN VS MEN

Because the British authorities didn't believe in women doing the same jobs as men, or being given equal pay, Joan had to be recruited as a "cleric" or secretary, on a much lower salary than Alan. She was eventually promoted to "linguist", but this was still a lie as she was codebreaking alongside the men.

The Dastardly Dolphin

In early 1940, the different Enigmas used by each branch of the enemy's military were divided up between the chief cryptanalysts who each took over one of the various "Huts".

Gordon Welchman

Dilly Knox

Gordon Welchman got the army and air force Enigmas in Hut 6 and Dilly Knox took the Italian naval Enigma. Alan, in Hut 8, got the biggest job of all: breaking the German naval Enigma traffic, codenamed "Dolphin". These were messages sent to and from the German U-boats (submarines): terrifying stealth vessels, which were taking out British ship after British ship on a daily basis, killing troops and sinking vital supplies. This, then, was an urgent task, but one everyone dreaded, as it had proved impossible, so far. Not Alan, though. He was happy to take the impossible on, mostly because it meant he could work alone, which was just how he liked it.

What made this Enigma so fiendish was threefold:

1. Instead of five wheels to choose from, this machine had eight, meaning the number of possible wheel arrangements rose from sixty to 336.

2. Instead of being fixed, the reflector also had twenty-six possible starting positions.

3. Instead of just using Enigma to send a message key, the navy encrypted one three-letter message key on Enigma, then made up a second three-letter key, added that to the first encryption, and then encrypted both using something called "bigram tables".

For example, the message key BOB might recode as DAN. The operator would write that down, and then above it, write down their own three-letter key, such as POB. That would look like this:

P	O	B
D	A	N

The operator would then take out their bigram table (which listed paired letters, and then gave new pairs for each) and re-encrypt the vertical pairs. So PD might be replaced with MO, OA with TH, BN with ER to give the new key:

M	T	E
O	H	R

So, this key "MOTHER" is what would then be sent by Morse code. At the other end, the operator would reverse the procedure, again using bigram tables and Enigma.

More cribbing

To solve the Dolphin messages, cribs were essential again.

As well as WETTER, Alan worked out that the word FORT was often used, an abbreviation of "FORTSETZUNG", which meant "continuation of the previous message". Not only that, but this would then be followed by the number of the previous message, spelled out in full in German. For example, a continuation of message 3345 would become FORTDREIDREIVIERFUNF. This gave Alan a much longer crib to check. But there was a problem: cribs relied on having a supply of already decrypted messages, which he didn't.

Luckily Alan had other tricks up his sleeve.

Banburismus

His next stroke of genius was to use a kind of frequency analysis, revealing where the same letter appeared. As in the much simpler Caesar shift, if two messages were encrypted on the same settings the cipher texts would be slightly more similar than completely random letters, because some letters are used more often than others. He worked out that if he lined up two pieces of cipher text, the match would be one in seventeen rather than one in twenty-six.

To test this, messages were punched as holes on to sheets of paper pre-typed with the alphabet in identical rows. These sheets were slid across each other until the largest number of holes lined up (the more holes, the more the chance of a match). This allowed some of the eight possible wheels to be eliminated with a small degree of certainty. Alan christened the method "Banburismus" after the nearby town of Banbury where the sheets of paper were made. To most of us, Banburismus might seem no better than "following a hunch". But Alan knew from maths that this kind of small "probability" – the difference between one in seventeen and one in twenty-six – could make a big impact. In the case of Banburismus, it was a difference that could save lives.

The problem was that, without a bigram table,

Banburismus was effectively useless. What Alan and his team needed was a "pinch".

BANBURISMUS AND THE BRAIN

Research suggests our brains use a method similar to Banburismus when confronted with competing sensory information, for example: it's hot/it's cold. The brain uses Banburismus to weigh up the evidence before making a decision.

The James Bond Pinch

A "pinch" was the term used to describe the capture of code books, bigram tables and even Enigma machines from the enemy. Whenever the British managed to attack a ship they would launch a boarding party who would search for these vital items. Unfortunately, pinches were few and far between as the Germans were clever and threw everything they could overboard.

That didn't deter the British though, especially one man in particular: Commander Ian Fleming from Naval Intelligence, better known now as the creator of the fictional spy, James Bond.

A regular visitor to Bletchley, Fleming had struck upon an ingenious idea. His plan was to use a captured German bomber and a "tough crew" of five people, dressed in *Luftwaffe* uniform, with fake blood and bandages, preferably speaking word-perfect German, and then crash the plane into the English Channel. He guessed that the German navy, seeing one of their own planes struck down, would come to the rescue. The British crew would then shoot the Germans, dump them overboard, and navigate the boat back to England, along with all its cipher treasure. The plan was codenamed "Operation Ruthless" and, though it sounds as far-fetched as a Bond plot, the authorities gave it the go-ahead. Alan was thrilled – breaking Dolphin was now within reach.

However, rather unlike a Bond plot, the operation had to be cancelled due to a lack of suitable target German boats. Alan was reportedly furious, complaining the authorities didn't seem to understand the importance of a "pinch" and that without one there was no hope of deciphering Dolphin for months and months, if ever.

Luckily for Turing, his bosses, and for all of us, there were other ways to get hold of the necessary material, and ones that didn't involve such cinematic plots.

JAMES BOND

A version of the Enigma even made it into the 1957 James Bond novel *From Russia With Love*, as the "Spektor" encryption machine.

The Somali Pinches

A British destroyer, HMS *Somali*, managed to score hits on a German trawler called *Krebs*. A boarding party searched *Krebs* and, though the vital bigram tables had been thrown overboard along with the Enigma machine, the crew found its wheels in a locked box, along with documents giving the plugboard and wheel settings for a whole month. This was a landmark pinch. Using the codebooks, Alan actually managed to reconstruct the bigram tables!

Inspired, another Bletchley worker, Harry Hinsley, had the brilliant idea of targeting weather ships, which were only lightly armed and operated alone. This made them easy – or easier – prey. As luck would have it, he happened to know the whereabouts of one such ship – the *München* – from previous decrypts. Again, the *Somali* swung into action, scoring hits on the *München* and sending in a search party who found the plugboard and wheel settings for another month.

At last, Alan was in and messages could be read within hours of being sent. This was a real victory, and one worth rewarding.

HMS Somali

A Letter to Churchill

Alan, Hugh Alexander and Gordon Welchman were summoned to Whitehall to be thanked personally by Churchill, each receiving a bonus of £200 (which was more than half a year's fellowship salary for Alan). This was brilliant in itself, but Alan, being Alan, saw in Churchill's gratitude another advantage.

Despite their success, the cryptanalysts were coming up against problems from people higher up the command, who were refusing to fund their vital work properly. So, Alan and his friends wrote to Churchill asking for help. Specifically, Alan asked for:

1. Twenty women clerks to work on night shifts.

2. Twenty trained typists to help them decode the increase in traffic.

3. A "body" of Wrens to operate the Bombes.

The letter was to be hand-delivered to Whitehall by their Hut 6 colleague, the *Times* chess correspondent Stuart Milner-Barry, who joked that he was the most expendable of all of them. The letter made it (and Stuart made it back). But more importantly, it had met its target. Churchill replied telling those in charge to make sure Alan and the others had everything they needed.

SILENCE IS GOLDEN

Churchill called Turing and his colleagues "the geese that laid the golden eggs but never cackled", a reference to their silence about their secret work.

DELILAH AND THE COLOSSUS

Tunny

The Bombe, of course, despite its incredible achievements, wasn't the end of the war story by a long chalk.

The Germans, whilst still fairly oblivious to the level of British interception, were constantly on the lookout for ways to make their messages more secure. In early 1942, they upped the number of wheels in place on the naval Enigma to four, taking the number of initial wheel settings up to 456,976 and the number of overall settings to be checked to a staggering 60 million million million million. This sneaky switchover put Hut 8 into "blackout" for months and, worse, meant the number of British ships being sunk started to rise again.

They'd also been using a new, even more

complicated encryption machine to send messages about long-term strategy between the *Wehrmacht* or "high command", including to and from Hitler himself. This machine was called the *Lorenz*, or a "Tunny" machine to the British. The Tunny machine used twelve wheels at once and, rather than relying on Morse code, sent its binary-based cipher straight out into the airwaves via teleprinter. It was an entirely new system, and as such it needed an entirely new method, machine and man to crack it.

Tunny machine

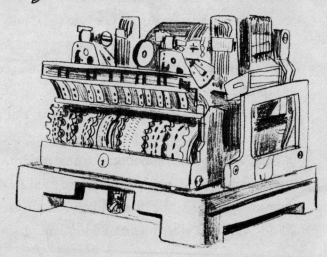

WHAT'S A TUNNY?

The Brits didn't know what kind of machine was being used to send these new messages, hence the "Tunny" nickname, tunny being a kind of fish – appropriate for naval messages.

Turingery

Finally, Bletchley Park called on Max Newman, Alan's old Cambridge mentor. Left off the list of "men of the professor type" at first, now he was installed at Bletchley in what was to become known as the "Newmanry". And, of course, Alan would be key in helping him.

Alan's job was to find a way to work out the twelve-wheel details. His solution was a return to the concept of probability, using insight and intuition or, as Alan put it, what you "felt in your bones" to guess the most likely combination. The method was nicknamed "Turingismus" or "Turingery". And it worked, at least for a while, but, as ever, the Germans tightened up security. This time, a man called Bill Tutte, who had originally worked out the setup of the machine, tried a new method, but one that still incorporated the idea behind Alan's Turingery. It worked, but the trouble was it took so long to do the calculations by hand, it was virtually pointless. What they needed was a machine.

This time, though, construction wasn't Alan's responsibility. Instead, that fell to an unassuming engineer called Tommy Flowers, while Alan found himself not just in a new job, but a new country.

Back to America

The United States had joined the war after the Japanese attacked their Hawaiian naval base, Pearl Harbor, in December 1941. Now, the Brits and the "Yanks" were collaborating, and Alan's next job was a secret mission to find out what they were doing in terms of breaking German messages. So, having handed control of Hut 8 over to Hugh Alexander, and said goodbye to the Newmanry, for the second time in his career Alan set sail for America.

This time, his passage wasn't just cramped – he was the only civilian on board a ship packed full of troops – but it was downright dangerous too. With Hut 8 still battling the new four-wheel Enigma, the Atlantic was a bloodbath. Despite this evident peril, Alan managed to make it to New York but again, received a less-than-cheery welcome.

Alan had been told by the Foreign Office to take no documents with him other than what was in his "diplomatic bag". But when he arrived in port, immigration officers said his papers weren't good enough – he had no evidence of any orders, or in fact any connection to the Foreign Office at all. At one point they debated detaining him in the internment camp on Ellis Island. Eventually, he was let in, and allowed to go ahead with his business at Bell Laboratories, which was constructing the secret machines. But they didn't trust him either, and it took six weeks of arguing between the top British and American generals before Bell Labs would let him in. Finally, though, the doors opened, and Alan could fulfil his mission.

ELLIS ISLAND

Ellis Island was usually the immigration gateway in New York to the US until 1954. But, during World War Two, the Americans began rounding up German, Italian and Japanese people, as well as other potentially suspicious foreigners, and kept them locked up there.

Speech Encryption

Alan's American mission was two-fold. First, he was to check over the production of an American version of the Bombe. Then, he was to look into their work on speech encryption and decryption.

Decrypting supposedly secure "text" messages in the war had been the first crucial step, but now the British and Americans were fighting a battle of their own to stop the Germans listening in on the British prime minister, Churchill, and American president, Roosevelt. The problem was, even though their "voice messages" were being sent via a sort of "scrambler" (which jumbled up the words so they made no sense unless you had a de-scrambler), this was no longer secure. What's more, the new American version weighed fifty tonnes, needed thirteen people to work it and still emitted a sort of horrible screech. Alan knew he could make something better. Something smaller and more portable, so, like the Enigma, it might be moved around.

So, just a few months later, with the seeds of several ideas in his head, Alan set sail for home, on the *Empress of Scotland*. His passage was no less frightening. Just nine days earlier a sister ship, the *Empress of Canada*, had been sunk. And she wasn't the only one. In the first few weeks of March 1943, three "wolf packs" of U-boats – thirty-six in all – had fought against three British convoys, sinking ninety-seven merchant ships, sending their men and their cargoes to the bottom of the sea. But, thankfully, this battle was to be the last.

The blackout at Bletchley was over and in May 1943, after suffering terrible losses, the Germans abandoned U-boat operations in the Atlantic completely. The timing was right for Alan to move on.

Delilah

Alan's move was literal. He said goodbye to Bletchley and was installed in nearby Hanslope Park, home of the "Radio Security Service", where he would be able to build his machine, this time doing some of the work himself.

Alan, it turned out, was not the tidiest of engineers. According to his assistant, Don Bayley, there were wires trailing everywhere and, as fast as he soldered bits on, others would fall off. But still Alan was proud of his creation, offering a prize for the best name, finally settling on "Delilah", named after the biblical character who had deceived Samson. Alongside working on Delilah, though, Alan found he had time to ponder another project.

Back at Bell Labs in America, Alan had found

a fellow computing enthusiast called Claude Shannon, who had studied neurology as well as maths. Together they discussed the possibility of an "electric brain" or "thinking machine". A machine that didn't just follow orders, but one that could, like our own brains, "learn". And what's more, one that didn't have to be fed by infinite tape, like the Universal Machine, but which could store things in an internal "memory". Now, Alan turned to Bayley and began discussing how to turn that storage into a reality.

Meanwhile, back at Bletchley, another machine was being constructed.

THE GINGER CAT

Alan also left his digs at the Crown and moved into a cottage with his colleague (and former King's student, of course) Robin Gandy – who had suggested "Delilah". They also adopted a stray ginger cat, who often accompanied the pair for long walks in the country.

Tommy Flowers

Tommy Flowers cut a very different figure to Alan. Born in rented rooms in East London, Flowers was a working-class son of a cockney, whose granddad had been a poacher, and grandma a cleaner. Despite this humble upbringing, Flowers had been determined to become an engineer since he was a small boy. When told he was about to get a baby sister, he said he'd much rather have a set of Meccano.

He may not have got the toy he wanted, but he did get to live

Tommy Flowers

his dream, becoming an engineering apprentice, before teaching himself electronics and joining the General Post Office (GPO), which, in those days, wasn't just in charge of letters, but also telephone services and radio, too. Having proved himself working on Fighter Command radar systems, which revealed exactly where German aircraft were flying, he was summoned to Bletchley. He was originally recruited to help Alan on another project, and Alan had clearly been impressed so, when Max Newman was looking for someone to build the machine to crack Tunny, Alan didn't hesitate in recommending him.

Flowers was undoubtedly the man for the job. Not only was he skilled in electronics, which the machine would need to be up to speed, he was also undeterred by the lack of support from certain quarters in Bletchley, who didn't believe his machine would actually work. Up until then, they'd been depending on another machine design called the "Heath Robinson", named after the cartoonist and illustrator, William Heath Robinson, who drew elaborate mechanical inventions which were supposed to achieve simple tasks. The problem was that the Heath Robinson relied on mechanical relay switches, which were very slow: a fact that Flowers recognized immediately on seeing it. He knew it needed electronic valves instead, which could switch a thousand times more quickly. Unfortunately, the officials in charge didn't believe him and so he ended up building the machine in secrecy in his own lab, even ploughing a thousand pounds of his own savings into it. It was worth it, though.

The Colossus

The machine took him ten months – an incredible feat, given it would have likely taken several years even if a war hadn't been taking place. But it was an incredible machine. Dwarfing even the enormous Bombe, it was as big as a room, and weighed a tonne. No wonder then that it quickly became known as the Colossus, which comes from the ancient Greek for "giant statue".

What's even more incredible is that the

Colossus was delivered to Bletchley on the back of an open lorry – a fact that seems astounding given the machine's secrecy. Not that it was easy to tell from the outside what was going on inside. And what was going on inside was genius. In its first test it successfully decoded a message so quickly the officials, who had changed their tune, swiftly ordered ten more machines. With these Colossi soon up and running, and an eleventh commissioned, Alan's inspiration, Tutte's algorithms and Flowers's build were cracking Tunny messages left, right and centre. But, brilliant though that was, that wasn't the most amazing thing about it. What was almost mind-blowing was that here was the world's first electronic computer.

Admittedly, it wasn't quite a computer in our sense, or even Alan's – it had no facility for stored programs; instead instructions were inputted manually using plugs and switches – but, crucially, Flowers had shown that large-scale electronic computing wasn't just a pipe dream. Alan's "thinking machine" was no longer just a clever theory; it was within grasp. And within a matter of months now, not decades.

Alan's Delilah, meanwhile, never saw the light of day. By the time it was finished, the call for speech encryption was no longer urgent. The war was coming to an end and, with it, Alan's career as a codebreaker.

The Colossus

The End of the War

It's hard to say exactly how many lives Alan's work saved, but rough estimates claim that cracking the Enigma shortened the war by between two and four years, preventing the deaths of many millions of people. Whatever the final number, Alan's impact is unquestionable.

But, of course, no one was to know about any of this in Alan's lifetime. At the end of the war, the Bombes were dismantled and the Colossi broken up. And, though he was awarded the OBE by King George VI in 1946, for "wartime services", no one knew what those services actually were. As far as Alan's family were concerned, he'd spent the war working in "radio operations". As far as his fellow mathematicians were concerned, he'd simply wasted six years when he could have been publishing more ground-breaking papers (though surely, they'd be more generous today, knowing what we do now of Alan's valiant war effort).

Still, even without the kudos of breaking Enigma to his name, Alan had more innovative ideas in him to impress the academics yet. Before he was released back to "civvy street" though, he had one last military mission.

SALVAGING COLOSSUS

Although most of the Bletchley equipment was smashed or dismantled, Max Newman managed to salvage the parts of a Colossus, and take it with him to his new job in Manchester.

The Last Post

The war over, Alan and Tommy Flowers were despatched to Germany to see for themselves the German encryption equipment used throughout the war. The absurdity of this is that, when an officer proudly showed them a Lorenz machine, neither could admit they'd not only seen one before but together had helped crack it.

What was more significant about the trip, though, was the agreement struck between Alan and Flowers about their next move.

In June 1945, just before he'd left for Germany, Alan had met up with a man called

John Womersley, who showed him a report on an American computing machine called the "Electronic Discrete Variable Automatic Computer" or "EDVAC" for short. The document was game-changing. The EDVAC built on Alan's ideas from his old paper *On Computable Numbers* as well as the *Electronic Numerical Integrator and Computer*, or "ENIAC", which had been used to work on some of the most secret equations of the war: the maths used in designing the atomic bomb. Like a Bombe, it couldn't store a program, and had to be configured with switches and cables. But, crucially, the ENIAC didn't do just one thing. It was multi-purpose, or, to put it another way, universal. And so, too, would be the EDVAC.

But this was just the beginning. Because Womersley, who had even once planned his own "Turing machine" using a telephone and was a long-time admirer of Alan, happened to be in charge of the National Physics Laboratory in London. As such, he had the authority and funds to build a British version of the EDVAC. What's more, he wanted Alan to do it.

Here was everything Alan could have hoped for. The war was over, and he and Flowers had a new prize in sight. They would go to the NPL and work together to beat the Yanks and build the world's first electronic, stored-program computer.

THE WORLD'S FIRST COMPUTER

For years, history books claimed ENIAC was the world's first computer. Of course, this was only because no one outside Bletchley knew about Colossus until decades later.

THE ACE VERSUS THE MANCHESTER BABY

The ACE Race

In September 1945, Alan joined the NPL and immediately began drawing up his own computer design, focusing on speed and size of memory, which he knew would be crucial. The design, dubbed the "Automatic Computing Engine" or "ACE" (named by Womersley in honour of Babbage's Analytical Engine), ran to forty-eight pages, with fifty-two diagrams and tables. It would cost a whopping £100,000, no small potatoes given the Bombe had cost just £6,500 a few years previously. This would be worth it, though, its massive capacity outdoing anything the Americans were thinking of. Or so Alan told the man who held the purse-strings, Sir Charles Galton Darwin. Darwin said he would think about it. (Of course, Alan couldn't tell him about its predecessor, the secret Colossus, or Darwin may have been convinced more quickly.)

In any case, progress on Alan's design was slow, mainly because the enormous memory required hundreds of "mercury delay" lines, and engineers were struggling to get a single one to work. Meanwhile, an eager new American recruit called Harry Huskey, who had worked on the ENIAC, began working on a version of his own which would be smaller and easier to build, which he then showed to Alan. Despite the clever modifications, Alan was quite put out and refused to work with Huskey. His decision seemed justified when Sir Charles finally gave the green light to Alan's design and demanded Huskey stop on the other version.

At this point, morale at the NPL, already wavering, sank to a new low. Huskey went back to America, while Alan, still awaiting a working relay line, went on sabbatical, hoping that by the time he came back everything would be sorted. The problem was that Alan and the ACE engineers were not the only ones battling to build a computer. As well as the Americans, led by an old Princeton colleague of Alan's called John von Neumann, another British team was in the race, and threatening to pull far, far ahead.

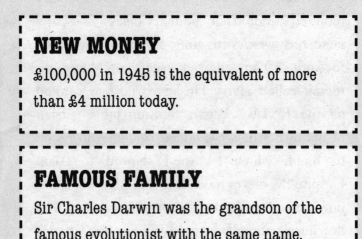

NEW MONEY

£100,000 in 1945 is the equivalent of more than £4 million today.

FAMOUS FAMILY

Sir Charles Darwin was the grandson of the famous evolutionist with the same name.

Max Newman and the Manchester Baby

After the war, when Alan went to the NPL, his mentor and Bletchley colleague, Max Newman, had smuggled a dismantled Colossus with him and taken it to Manchester University, where he set up the "Computing Machine Laboratory" to build a machine that could rival the ACE. Crucially, the "Baby", as it became known, didn't rely on expensive and slow relays for its memory but on the cheaper cathode ray – the same technology used in old televisions, and an idea mooted by Alan many years before.

In fact, the Manchester Baby, or "Manchester Brain" as it was sometimes known, owed rather a large debt to Alan. The engineer, Tom Kilburn, learned all he knew about computer design from a series of lectures given in London in 1946. The speaker, at the Adelphi Hotel on the Strand, had been none other than Alan.

Later in life, Kilburn said he couldn't remember where he got the idea from, but the fact remains that Alan had a hand in the Baby even before it was built, with the first design following Turing's principles clearly.

Alan, meanwhile, was up to something else entirely.

Alan the Olympian

This new pastime was nothing to do with maths or machines. This time, Alan had taken up long-distance running. In fact, this was not a new hobby. Alan had enjoyed running as a boy, joking that his ability came from avoiding the ball in hockey. At Bletchley it's claimed he ran nearly fifty miles along the Grand Union Canal when he was needed at meetings in London, and at NPL often ran the fifteen or so miles to visit Tommy Flowers at his lab in Dollis Hill. At the time, that may have seemed to some as a little eccentric. But not any more.

He was recruited to the local Walton Athletic Club, having run past them when they were out training, and now he was taking running rather seriously. So seriously that, in 1946, he won the three-mile Club Championship. Then, the following year, he came fifth in the Amateur Athletic Association Championship marathon.

Today, his time of two hours and forty-six minutes might seem rather snail-paced, but back then it put him in with a real chance of competing at the 1948 Olympics, which were to be held in London. In the end, a leg injury meant he missed out on a place on the British team, but his try-out time was only minutes off those of the eventual medal places, proving he had real athletic talent as well as brains.

Friends Reunited

Though he was enjoying his sabbatical, Alan's frustration at the delays in ACE were mounting. When he popped back to the NPL to check how things were progressing, he found that nothing had changed. Venting this anger in a conversation with Max Newman, his former rival saw an obvious and brilliant solution. He offered Alan a job in Manchester. To the shock and, one assumes, anger of Sir Charles, Alan accepted.

Was Alan's decision the right one? Although the ACE did eventually get made, it wasn't until May 1950. However, as Alan had planned, it trumped its rivals in terms of speed and memory. It also became commercially successful in the form of the "DEUCE", which was one of the earliest electronic computers to go on the market (although "success" is relative, as back then sales were only around ten a year). The first portable desk-side computer, the Bendix G15, was also based on Alan's ACE design. But by that point, Alan was long gone and far away. Two hundred miles to the northwest to be precise, in a move that was to mark the last dramatic chapter in his life story.

MOSAIC

Flowers, meanwhile, had built his own version, which eventually became the "MOSAIC" – a top secret computer used in the Cold War.

Alan in Manchester

Alan's life in Manchester was markedly different from his various digs in Cambridge and Bletchley. For a start, he bought his first home

– a semi-detached red-brick house in Wilmslow in Cheshire with the rather grand name of Hollymeade. He hired himself a housekeeper, too – Mrs Clayton – putting an end to his messy ways, as he no longer had to even think about tidying up himself, and thus wasting precious work time. He made friends with his neighbour, a fellow Sherborne boy, Roy Webb, and even babysat for Roy's son. Though Alan was rather a subversive babysitter. At one point he and the boy were to be found on the garage roof discussing whether God would catch a cold if he sat on the ground.

The Newmans also lived nearby, and Alan was a regular visitor to Max and his wife Lynn, who became a close friend, as well as their son, William. He continued his running too, in the Cheshire countryside. And, though he might have been tidier, many of his other eccentricities remained. According to William Newman, Alan once ran to their house in the early hours of the morning to invite them to dinner. Realizing when he got there that they were probably all asleep, he scratched his invitation on a leaf with a stick and posted it through the letterbox.

The fact was, Alan was happy in Manchester. He had a home, he had a social life, he had countryside in which to run. But most importantly, at long last, he had his computer.

Alan's Baby

The race to build the world's first stored-program electronic computer was finally won on 21 June 1948, with the birth of the Manchester Baby. Three months later, Alan arrived.

His official title was deputy director, but in fact there was no director and he was pretty much left in charge and to his own devices, which was fine by Alan. He began by designing a programming system for the computer, and a series of improvements, including a proper input and output – until then, programming had been done by a series of switches and output was no more than a screen displaying a series of dots. Instead, Alan used teleprinter tape – the same system used by Colossus.

But the Baby was just that: an infant. And Alan knew the computer would need to keep growing and changing if it was to keep up. And so, with Alan at the helm, the Manchester Baby was rebuilt in a newer, faster, and far more commercial form: the Mark 1.

The Manchester Mark 1

The Mark 1 was ready for manufacture by Ferranti in 1949, and the plan was that, in the meantime, Alan would work on an operation manual and some basic programs.

Manchester Mark 1.

Programming the Mark 1 was still a long way off today's comparatively quick and easy process. Back then each instruction, consisting of twenty binary digits, was fed into the machine on teleprinter tape. But, painstaking though it was, the important thing was that it worked.

The Manchester Mark 1 was switched on in February 1951 and fulfilled and even surpassed everyone's expectations, as well as exceeding the performance of the Pilot ACE. Part of that performance was its random number generator, ideal for computer games, and, strangely, for writing love letters. Here's an example (M.U.C. standing for Manchester University Computer):

Darling sweetheart
You are my avid fellow feeling. My affection
curiously clings to your passionate wish.
My liking yearns for your heart. You are my
wistful sympathy: my tender liking.
Yours beautifully
M.U.C.

What's really interesting about the letter is that, wordy though it is, it's actually quite hard to tell that this wasn't written by a human (albeit one who could use some lessons in concise writing). This concept – of a computer that might imitate a person – was to become Alan's next preoccupation. But not before mastering one of his favourite pastimes: chess.

MUSICAL HOOTER

Included in Alan's manual was a program that would get the computer to play music – something that few people had ever imagined possible. Alan's method involved the computer's warning "hooter" – an alarm that sounded whenever the machine needed attention.

By changing the frequency of the hooter, Alan worked out that you could make it sound as if it was playing a musical scale. This new musical range wasn't merely amusing; Alan used it practically, too, with different notes to

Computer Chess

Alan had long dreamt of a computer that could play chess, and had already written out the machine's specifications on paper with a friend, David Champernowne. Using this paper "machine" (dubbed the "TuroChamp"), Alan and David worked out what the machine's next move would be. This was a laborious process, taking half an hour instead of perhaps a few minutes or even seconds in real life. And it could only ever "think" about one move rather than predicting its opponent's moves and planning responses. But the thing worked. It even played a rival match against the "Machiavelli", a similar paper "machine" drawn up by Alan's old NPL colleague, Donald Michie, and another friend,

Shaun Wylie. The match was then played out by correspondence. No one knows who won this probably long-winded game, but that isn't really the point. What mattered was that the chess algorithm worked on paper. And now, with the Manchester Mark 1, the move to an electronic program was a real possibility. Again, the race between Manchester and the NPL was on.

In the event, Manchester won, although it wasn't Alan's program that took the prize. Instead, a Ferranti engineer called Dietrich Prinz beat everyone to it. His program was limited, but here was proof that a machine could, in one sense, "think". And if it could write love letters like a human, and play chess like a human, perhaps people might have to start thinking of it as a sort of human. This was the first glimpse of what we now know as artificial intelligence. It was a theory that had long fascinated Alan and was one that was to form the basis of one of his most famous achievements of all.

THE IMITATION GAME

Intelligent Machinery

If a computer can respond like a human; if it sounds like a human; if it effectively thinks like a human, then does it matter what it looks like?

This was Alan's driving question when he first put forward the idea of the "Imitation Game".

In a 1947 lecture, Alan was already imagining an age when machines would be able to "think" and "learn". He built on this in the 1948 paper, *Intelligent Machinery*, suggesting that:

> "MACHINERY MIGHT BE MADE TO SHOW INTELLIGENT BEHAVIOUR."

His big idea rested on the mechanisation of thought processes – the same principle used by the Bombe. This is the field we now know as

148

"artificial intelligence" and, to us, it may seem an obvious progression. But remember, back then computers were only just being invented.

Alan knew that the idea that a computer could effectively "think" wasn't just ground-breaking, it was controversial too. It suggested that humankind wasn't necessarily supreme in terms of intelligence any more. He knew it might also upset some religious people, admitting:

"ANY ATTEMPT TO CONSTRUCT SUCH MACHINES IS A SORT OF PROMETHEAN IRREVERENCE."

Prometheus was the mythical character who stole fire from the Greek gods and made human from clay. In other words, some might think that Alan was trying to play God himself.

The reaction to the Manchester Baby was already troubled. In 1949, the country's top brain surgeon, Sir Geoffrey Jefferson, had given a lecture rubbishing the computer. "Not until a machine can write a sonnet or a concerto [...]

could we agree that machine equals brain," he declared. "When we hear it said that wireless valves think, we may despair of language."

Alan, unsurprisingly, disagreed. He told the *Times*:

"THIS IS ONLY A FORETASTE OF WHAT IS TO COME, AND ONLY THE SHADOW OF WHAT IS GOING TO BE. I DO NOT SEE WHY IT SHOULD NOT ENTER ANY ONE OF THE FIELDS NORMALLY COVERED BY THE HUMAN INTELLECT, AND EVENTUALLY COMPETE ON EQUAL TERMS."

He did, however, admit that a sonnet written by machine might best be appreciated by another machine, rather than a human. Worried about the consequences of Alan's bravado, Max Newman himself wrote to the paper with details aimed at proving how dull the machine really was.

But in truth this "artificial brain" was far from dull, and only the start.

The Imitation Game

In 1950, Alan wrote another astonishing paper. This one was called *Computing Machinery and Intelligence* and proposed something called the "Imitation Game" (which we now know as the "Turing test"). This was an imaginary experiment involving a judge, a human competitor and a computer. The judge would ask the human and the computer a series of questions – then try to work out if the answers came from the human or the machine. Alan envisioned it like an oral exam, but with the answers written down (or it would have been too easy to tell a human voice from a robotic one).

This is Alan's example:

JUDGE: in the first line of your sonnet, which reads, "Shall I compare thee to a summer's day", would not "a spring day" do as well or better?

MACHINE: it wouldn't scan.

JUDGE: how about "a winter's day"? That would scan all right.

MACHINE: yes, but nobody wants to be compared to a winter's day.

The question for Alan wasn't so much "Can computers think?" but "Can computers pass the Turing test?" If they could pass the test, then that was the same as thinking, at least to Alan.

Turing Tests Today

A "Turing test" called the Loebner Prize is now held annually at Bletchley Park, run by the Society for the Study of Artificial Intelligence and Simulation of Behaviour. It's open to all ages and anyone can join in. Here's an example from the 2009 competition:

JUDGE: hi, how is it going?

COMPUTER: hello. How are you doing?

JUDGE: good. Who are you?

COMPUTER: well, I am studying engineering. That ought to give you an idea about who I am.

JUDGE: no, not really.

COMPUTER: I have a terrific yearning to know something more about experiments.

JUDGE: where are you from?

COMPUTER: I don't know, but don't forget I can't be in three places at once.

JUDGE: what city do you live in?

COMPUTER: what city? That's rather a tricky question. The trouble is, one city seems to be much like another.

JUDGE: not really. Where do you live?

COMPUTER: in the old dairy next to the river, I believe.

JUDGE: interesting, so you are a farmer then?

COMPUTER: well, if you ask a physiologist what I am, he won't say I'm a farmer. He'll say I consist mostly of water – enough to fill a large beer tun – plus some iron, phosphorus and lots of other prosaic ingredients.

JUDGE: weird answer to a simple question, wouldn't you say?

COMPUTER: I certainly would. Just watch me!

Does that sound almost-human to you? Perhaps not, but it's still a pretty impressive performance from a machine. And to be fair to Alan, in 1952, he did predict that it would be a hundred years before any computer could actually pass the Turing test. What he didn't predict is that in far less time, it would already have practical uses.

A reverse Turing test called the "CAPTCHA" is used on many websites to check that users are human and not "bots". Standing for "Completely Automated Public Turing test to tell Computers and Humans Apart", some are difficult-to-read warped words, others are images divided into sections with the user having to identify which sections include a certain object.

But back to the 1950s. And, knowing a passable Turing test was still a century off, perhaps, Alan turned his attention from artificial brains to real ones, for the last big discovery of his career.

TIGER STRIPES AND LEOPARD SPOTS

From Computers to Cows

Alan's move to biology might seem sudden, but it makes perfect Alan-sense.

From a very early age he had been as obsessed with the natural world as he was with other sciences. A famous sketch by his own mother depicts him staring at flowers on the ground in the middle of a school hockey match. Entitled *Hockey*, or *Watching the Daisies Grow*, it reveals not only Alan's lack of interest in team sports, but his future fascination. As a small boy, he'd also been given a copy of *Natural Wonders Every Child Should Know* by Edwin Tenney Brewster, a book that seemed to captivate him.

In adulthood, Alan's time was so taken up with maths and computing and codebreaking, he had little chance to investigate further, but then, in

1949, Alan became a member of the Ratio Club. This was an all-male society set up to debate the blurry area between maths, computing and biology, known as "cybernetics". While Alan gave talks on computing and intelligence, others held forth on topics like the size and shape of nerve fibres, and, interestingly, "pattern recognition".

Fibonacci and Friesians

Patterns in nature had been a particular interest of Alan's for many years, as far back as his Sherborne days. At first he found simple delight in finding Fibonacci numbers in plants and animals.

As mentioned on page 9, the Fibonacci sequence is a series of numbers where each new number is the sum of the previous two. Hence: 0, 1, 1, 2, 3, 5, 8, 13, 21, 34 and so on. As Alan and his one-time fiancée Joan Clarke both noted with interest and frequently discussed, the sequence appears everywhere in nature: in the leaf and petal arrangements in daisies, in the swirl of a pine cone, and in the spiral on a snail or even a cauliflower.

What Alan wanted to know was: how do these things grow? How did the information, which he knew was stored at cell level, get translated into the shape of a brain, into ears and a nose, the five points of a starfish, the stripes on a tiger, or the dappled black and white of a Friesian cow? In other words, what caused the process called "morphogenesis"?

The answer to Alan was, unsurprisingly, maths. And, just as he'd used it to decode Enigma, now he was going to use it to decode nature.

Morphogenesis

As a child staying with the Wards, Alan had listened time and again to Rudyard Kipling's *Just So Stories*. Kipling – a fellow foster child, though a much less happy one – explained the presence of phenomena like the spots on a leopard, the hump on a camel and the thick skin on a rhinoceros in far-fetched but entertaining stories. *How the Elephant got his Trunk*, for example, tells the tale of the Elephant's Child, an odd-looking creature with a "blackish bulgy nose as big as a boot", whose trunk only lengthens when it has to be hauled out of the jaws of a crocodile in the "great grey-green, greasy Limpopo river, all set about with fever trees".

One suspects that, even at the time, Alan knew this was twaddle, although he would have had no idea at that point of the real reason. By the age of forty, though, he had more than an inkling. Alan believed that growth and patterns and all these oddities like trunks and humps were caused by tiny fluctuations in the concentration of biochemicals, called "morphogens". These morphogens were being created, released and destroyed at different rates. And Alan knew how to explain "rates": equations. Using the Manchester Mark 1 computer, he came up with an equation to explain the development of a small round egg into something with distinct features.

His paper, *The Chemical Basis of Morphogenesis*, was published in August 1952. Like *Computing Machinery and Intelligence* and *On Computable Numbers* before it, it was cutting-edge stuff, going on to inspire work into solving stripes on zebras, the formation of feathers, even the branching pattern of lungs. Although at the time, some of the top biologists admitted the maths rather went over their heads.

What the biologists didn't know was that this paper was to be Alan's last major contribution to the world of science. Because, earlier that year, on 7 February, the day before he was due to give his talk at the Ratio Club on his findings, Alan had been arrested.

KIPLING

Like Alan, Kipling's parents lived in India while he stayed on the south coast of England with a foster family. Kipling, though, was appallingly mistreated, bullied by both Mrs Holloway, his foster mother, and her son.

INFAMY

The Strange Case of the Burglary

I t all started when Alan was burgled. He had come home to find his house broken into and some of his things missing:

2 medals
3 clocks
2 pairs of shoes
1 compass
1 watch
1 suitcase
1 part bottle of sherry
1 pair of trousers
1 shirt
1 pullover
1 case of fish knives and forks.

Together they were worth an estimated £50.10. Most of these, Alan could have lived without, but the watch had belonged to his father, Julius, who had died in 1947. And, although Alan never wore it, he was determined to see it returned. So, he reported the theft to the police, along with the name of one of the two men he suspected of breaking in: Harold Arthur Thacker.

This was when the police began to sense something else was up besides a standard break-in. How was it that Alan knew the name of one of the burglars? And why had he refused to tell the police exactly how he knew this, or name the informant (the person who had told him)?

The truth was that Alan knew the informant rather too well – he was Alan's boyfriend, Arnold Murray. And, a decade on from Alan's short-lived engagement to Joan, being gay remained a crime.

The Law on Homosexuality

While London's first gay pub opened its doors in the same year that Alan was born, this apparent openness was uncommon. The fact was, being gay was to remain a crime in Britain until 1967, and even then, it was still illegal for anyone under the age of twenty-one.

Unluckily for Alan, the burglary in 1952 coincided with an increased effort by authorities to clamp down on homosexuality. Over in America, the politician, Senator McCarthy, had added "homosexuals" to "communists" on his list of "enemies within". He wanted to "weed out" any gay men working in foreign policy, believing they would be easily blackmailed by the Russians (this was at the height of the Cold War, the long battle for supremacy between Russia and the United States). Back in London, the chief of Scotland Yard, Sir John Nott-Bower, was doing the same in the British government.

Over the next few years, as many as a thousand gay men were arrested and locked up, many of them "trapped" by undercover policemen who had pretended to be gay themselves. Alan, however, being innately honest, and entirely unashamed of his relationships, had rather walked into the arrest of his own accord.

CLAMPDOWN

The "clampdown" in Britain had kicked off after two British diplomats, Guy Burgess and Donald Maclean, both gay (and, incidentally, both former Cambridge University students) had defected to the Soviet Union.

Alan and Arnold

Alan met Arnold Murray in Manchester in January 1952, and they began a brief relationship, meeting at Alan's home, Hollymeade. Arnold, who was unemployed at the time, had been impressed by the place and boasted of his boyfriend's riches to an acquaintance called Harold Thacker in a "milk bar" (or café). Harold suggested they rob Alan. Arnold wanted nothing to do with it, he said. But too late: Harold was going to burgle Hollymeade, thinking that Alan was unlikely to go to the police, not wanting to draw attention to himself.

Unfortunately for everyone concerned, Harold was wrong. Alan did go to the police. On further questioning, he admitted why he had concealed the identity of his informant: because he was having an affair with him, a fact that Alan was unashamed about.

Unashamed he might rightly be, but he was also now implicated in another crime.

COCKLES AND MUSSELS

Alan even took to entertaining the police when they called round to the house, once playing "Cockles and Mussels" to them on his violin.

Alan's violin

The Trial

Many of Alan's close friends pleaded in court on Alan's behalf. But it was of no use. Harold Thacker was sentenced to "Borstal training" (Borstal being a sort of juvenile-offenders unit, named after the town in Kent where the first establishment appeared). Arnold Murray was "bound over to be of good behaviour for twelve months", meaning he was put on probation but avoided prison. But Alan's punishment was to be far more severe.

Alan was found guilty of "gross indecency" and given a choice of sentence. He could either go to prison, or submit to psychotherapy and hormone treatment, intended to "curb" or even "cure" his homosexuality. Alan, knowing he would lose his job, and more importantly, access to the computer if he went to prison, chose the treatment.

A PRISON CELL

While in custody before the trial, Alan joked that he rather liked the cells, as the lack of responsibility was like being back at school, with the prison warders no more than prefects. Though one suspects a long spell in prison might have been rather more distressing.

The Treatment

The hormone treatment forced on gay men was something called "stilboestrol" – a form of the female hormone oestrogen. The idea was that it would stop them wanting relationships with men by chemically controlling their sexual feelings. The reality was that it had a horrible list of side effects including – and, possibly worst of all for Alan – affecting the brain and the way one thought.

Alan, having been told these side effects were entirely reversible, bore the treatment with remarkable good humour. He began psychotherapy – a kind of intense investigation of thoughts and dreams – with Dr Franz

Greenbaum, who, along with his wife and daughters, became close friends. And, finally, having solved the problem of patterns on animals, Alan turned his attention to the pressing issue of the Fibonacci sequence in plants, a process called "phyllotaxis"; in other words, the spiral arrangement of leaves on a stem.

Despite this apparent acceptance, none of this could have been easy for Alan. These were the days before the Internet, and so public knowledge of the trial and sentence was limited. But the affair had been published in the local paper and a conviction for "gross indecency" was hardly a fantastic calling card. And, although Alan kept his job at the university, it ruled him out of ever working on codes and ciphers again, as at the time, gay men were considered, at least by the US Senate, to lack "emotional stability" and have weakened "moral fibre". And, like McCarthy's targets, they might be susceptible to blackmail. This was a huge disappointment to Alan, who had been helping former Bletchley pal, Hugh Alexander, on some ciphers and been offered £5,000 a year (a huge amount of money back then) to work for the new version of GC&CS: "GCHQ". He was also banned from travelling to America.

On top of that, while most of his close friends stood by Alan, others were warned off by police, and did as they were told. One of these was Alan's current running companion, a seventeen-year-old called Alan Garner, who would go on to become a famous children's author. Garner, obeying orders, ignored Alan when they happened to get on the same bus. It was the last time Garner saw his former friend alive. Because on 8 June 1954, just days before his forty-second birthday, Alan Turing was found dead at home. He had, it was declared, committed suicide.

UNFAIR TREATMENT

Treatment of the kind endured by Alan was reserved for people the court believed to be "mentally deficient", or of "unsound mind", as defined by the 1890 Lunacy Act. This in itself reveals the appalling way many people thought of homosexuality.

THE POISONED APPLE

The Facts

It was Mrs Clayton, the housekeeper, who found Alan's body. He was lying in bed, the covers pulled up, with a froth around his mouth and a strange smell of almonds in the air. Both the froth and the smell meant one thing: cyanide poisoning.

The police were called and searched the house, finding two jars of cyanide: one in his study, and another in his chest of drawers. Next to his bed was also an apple, with several bites missing. While the apple itself was never tested for cyanide, many believe Alan had used it to sweeten the bitter poison. Whatever the truth, its presence was certainly not insignificant.

The Poisoned Apple

As well as a love of running, Alan Turing and Alan Garner had bonded over their mutual fear of, and fascination with, the Disney film *Snow White and the Seven Dwarves*. While Alan Garner had been just seven at the time, Alan Turing was an adult when it released in 1938, but it captivated him, especially one scene: the wicked queen dipping the apple in poison. "Dip the apple in the brew, let the sleeping death seep through," she chanted. And so, too, did Alan, repeating the couplet again and again as he strode around King's College, and reviving it once more in conversation with Garner.

So, did Alan dip his apple in poison before taking a bite? Theories differ.

The Debate

While the coroner's verdict on Alan's death was suicide, history is rather more undecided.

Alan's mother, Sara, was firmly of the belief

that it was a terrible accident. She had warned him, she said, about his messy experiments and putting his fingers in his mouth. He had obviously swallowed some by mistake.

This was entirely plausible, of course. Like the child in the French cellar with his chemistry set, or the Sherborne boy with candles on his windowsill and "heaven-knows-what witches' brew", Alan had recently been conducting experiments at home in what he called his "nightmare room". One of these was, bizarrely, the gold-plating of teaspoons, a process that required a form of cyanide. It would have been easy for him to accidentally get the chemical on his fingers, or, as his friend, Don Bayley, contested, to put the apple down in a pool of it and then absent-mindedly take a bite.

However, the counter-theory to this is that Alan was well aware of his mother's opinions on his untidiness and careless attitude to experiments. He could have easily exploited this so that she would be able to tell herself it was an accident – far easier for a mother to accept than admitting her son was so unhappy, he had taken his own life, which at the time was not only a crime but considered a mortal sin. And why, if this was the case, did he die in his bedroom and not the nightmare room?

Alan had, admittedly, made a will recently, leaving money to his family and friends, as well as his housekeeper. Was this suspicious? Did he know he was going to die? Or was this just the sensible thing to do, given he now owned his own house?

Then there is the apple: yes, he had obsessed about the apple in *Snow White*, but he also ate one every night according to many people.

Other witnesses testified to his apparent happiness in the weeks and days leading up to his death. He had had dinner with his friends and neighbours, the Webbs, the previous Thursday, and been "merry", despite the fact that they were about to move. He'd bought theatre tickets. He'd accepted an invitation to a Royal Society function. His desk was in its habitual mess. He'd booked to use the computer that evening (the engineers waited up for him). His career was on a high, working on his new love, morphogenesis.

There was also, crucially, no suicide note.

But suicide cases, though all profoundly sad, are very different. And, even though the hideous hormone treatment had ended a year before, it's not hard to find the seeds of unhappiness in Alan's life following his arrest and conviction. He'd apparently visited a fortune-teller a few months earlier on a visit to the Blackpool Pleasure Beach with the Greenbaums, with worrying results.

When he was a child, Alan had been taken to see a fortune-teller at a church fete who told him he would be a genius. This time his predicted fate wasn't so positive. According to one of the Greenbaums' daughters, Barbara, Alan emerged from the tent pale and clearly shaken. Though he would never divulge exactly what he'd been told, he did admit it was awful and that he was very unhappy. This was the last time the Greenbaums saw him before his death.

Finally, a theory has been put forward that Alan was murdered. Why, the question goes, were his shoes left outside his room, as if awaiting a servant to polish them when, according to his housekeeper, he had never done this before?

Shoes aside, the theory isn't entirely implausible. After all, Alan had been the man behind the Bletchley breaking of Enigma and as such, his mind was potentially useful in the continuing Cold War. Maybe he knew too much about too much?

The best answer to all of this comes from Alan's own nephew, Sir Dermot Turing. Perhaps, he suggests, given the impossibility of ever finding the answer to this final problem, we should celebrate Alan's life rather than pry too hard into his death.

SUICIDE ACT 1961

Suicide was a crime until the Suicide Act 1961, and anyone who attempted it could be prosecuted, or, in the case of those who succeeded, their families could be prosecuted instead. Thankfully our understanding of mental health along with our empathy has improved a lot since then.

Burial

After the funeral, Alan's ashes were scattered at Woking Crematorium, just as his father's had been. Perhaps Bletchley would have been a more suitable resting place. But, of course, none of his family knew about that part of his life, and they wouldn't for another two decades.

FAME AT LAST

The Secret's Out

In 1940, the mathematician, Godfrey Harold Hardy, declared, "Real mathematics has no effects on war. No one has yet discovered any warlike purpose to be served by the theory of numbers or relativity, and it seems unlikely that anyone will do so for many years."

Of course, he couldn't have known what was going on behind the gates at Bletchley Park, and wouldn't find out in his lifetime. The Official Secrets Act kept everyone's mouths glued shut for three decades after the war ended. Then, in the mid-seventies, the government "declassified" the information, meaning people were free to talk. The first to do so was Frederick Winterbotham, who had been in charge of "Ultra" intelligence during the war. His book *The Ultra Secret* lifted the lid on the story of Bletchley and Enigma. This was swiftly followed by *Bodyguard of Lies* by Anthony Cave Brown, which mentioned Alan several times.

All bets were now off, and the Bletchley secrets came tumbling out in book after book, in TV programmes, even in films, so that now, this once dark corner of espionage is perhaps the most brightly illuminated of all in history, with Alan the star at the centre of it all. Even though the job hadn't been one he'd really even wanted. Alan once wrote to a friend:

"MY AMBITION IS TO BECOME A DON AT KING'S, I AM AFRAID IT MAY BE MORE AMBITION THAN PROFESSION THOUGH. I MEAN IT IS NOT VERY LIKELY I SHALL EVER BECOME ONE."

Though he was probably dismissed as modest at the time, Alan was right in the end, instead becoming lauded for so much more. But for Alan, these wartime heroics were only part of the tale. There was another strand of Alan's story that needed rewriting.

An Apology and Pardon

In 1954, Alan had died a convicted man, found guilty of something that, forty years later, was no longer a crime. It was high time to put right that wrong.

Following more changes in the law, in August 2009 a British computer programmer called John Graham-Cumming started a petition asking the government to apologize for the way it had treated Alan. In a few weeks it gained more than 30,000 signatures and, the following month, Prime Minister Gordon Brown finally issued a heartfelt apology:

It is thanks to men and women who were totally committed to fighting fascism, people like Alan Turing, that the horrors of the Holocaust and of total war are part of Europe's history and not Europe's present.

So, on behalf of the British government, and all those who live freely thanks to Alan's work, I am very proud to say: we're sorry. You deserved so much better.

Turing's Law

∙∙

Alan did deserve better. He deserved real recognition. And now he had the backing of the public to make sure he got it. More petitions were drawn up and fellow scientist, Stephen Hawking, wrote to the *Daily Telegraph* asking the new prime minister, David Cameron, to support an official "pardon", which is one step up from an apology, clearing Alan of ever having committed a crime.

An MP called Christopher Chope objected to the idea, but the prime minister wasn't to be put off. In the end, he bypassed Parliament completely and went straight to the Queen, who signed a royal pardon on Christmas Eve 2013. Even better, in 2016, this exoneration was extended to the thousands and thousands of other gay men who'd been prosecuted simply for being themselves. This is now known as the Alan Turing law.

Though many agree this will never make up for the appalling hormone treatment Alan endured, or the ban from working on ciphers again, at least today we're able to pay tribute to his brilliance and heroism, and in so many places around the world.

TURING TODAY

Bletchley

There are Turing exhibitions and tributes throughout the UK, but perhaps the best of all is Bletchley Park itself, now preserved as a museum of codebreaking. You can see for yourself what Hut 8 was like during the war, look at real Enigma and "Tunny" machines and have a go at decoding. You can even see Alan's much-loved teddy bear, Porgy, and the infamous tea mug, chained to the radiator.

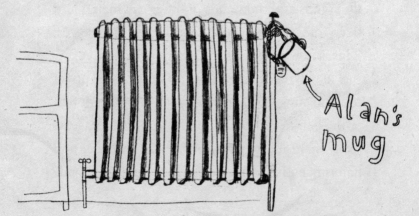

Alan's mug

Government Communication Headquarters (GCHQ)

Bletchley closed its gates to cipher work when the last workers left after the war in 1945, but Britain still has a codebreaking centre, now known as the Government Communication Headquarters. This time, though, its location is no longer a secret – it's in Cheltenham, with smaller sites in Manchester, Cornwall and North Yorkshire. And they're all kept very busy. Today's secret ciphers are even more complicated than Enigma's and, with the threat of terrorism on the rise, mathematicians are more vital than ever to help crack them.

GCHQ

You can't visit GCHQ, for obvious reasons, but you can read about it here: www.gchq.gov.uk

The National Museum of Computing

Right next door to Bletchley Park is the National Museum of Computing, where you can find out more about Alan's ground-breaking work on computers, as well as see a reconstructed Bombe and a Colossus.

The Alan Turing Institute

The British Library in London has its own Alan Turing Institute of data science and artificial intelligence. This conducts research, trains leaders in science, and generally tries to continue Alan's work and keep it in the public's imagination. You can go to fascinating lectures there, and also view an Enigma machine at its entrance.

The Turing Memorial

Perhaps one of the most moving tributes is

the *Alan Turing Memorial* in Sackville Park in Manchester. This is a bronze statue of Alan sitting on a wooden bench, with the infamous apple in his hand. The plaque reads "Father of Computer Science, Mathematician, Logician, Wartime Codebreaker, Victim of Prejudice". Behind him on the bench itself is the message "Founder of Computer Science" as if coded by an Enigma machine: "IEKYF RQMSI ADXUO KVKZC GUBJ". Although whether an Enigma was really used is disputed because it would mean the letter "U" had been encrypted as itself, which, as you should know by now, would be an impossibility.

On top of this, you can spot both Alan Turing Road in Loughborough, Alan Turing Way in Manchester, and another Alan Turing Road in Guildford in Surrey, close to where his parents moved in 1927. There's also another statue at the University of Surrey, the Turing Room at King's College, the Alan Turing Auditorium at Stanford University in America, and many more.

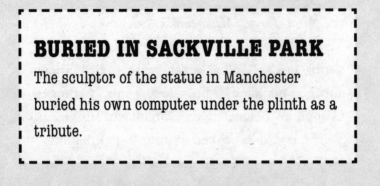

BURIED IN SACKVILLE PARK

The sculptor of the statue in Manchester buried his own computer under the plinth as a tribute.

Alan Turing Memorial, Sackville Park.

Turing on TV

In 2019, Alan Turing was voted the BBC's Icon of the Twentieth Century, after an impassioned speech by TV presenter, Chris Packham.

Turing Everywhere

Of course, Alan, who famously kept his OBE in his toolbox, may have shied away from this newfound fame.

So, perhaps the easiest way to pay tribute to Alan is to think of him every time you Google something, in fact every time you use a smartphone, or a laptop or a tablet. Because it's thanks to him these ingenious devices exist at all. Perhaps it's thanks to him and his heroic wartime codebreaking that many of us even exist at all.

So, what better way to finish this story than this:

Thanks, Alan.

TIMELINE OF ALAN TURING'S LIFE

1912 Alan Mathison Turing is born in Little Venice, London. His parents soon depart for India, leaving him and his brother with foster parents for the next few years.

1922 Sent to Hazelhurst Prep in Sussex, where he is unhappy.

1926 Sent to Sherborne School in Dorset. Struggles in some subjects, and is bullied by other boys.

1929 Meets Christopher Morcom, who inspires him to work harder. Christopher and Alan take Cambridge scholarship exams. Alan fails. Christopher succeeds, but dies of TB just weeks later in February 1930.

1930 Alan takes the Cambridge scholarship exam again and is offered a place at King's.

1931 Alan begins his career at King's, gaining a first-class degree in mathematics, and becoming a "fellow" in 1935, the first of his cohort.

1936 Publishes his seminal paper, *On Computable Numbers*, which proposes a "Universal Machine" to replace the human computer. Moves to Princeton to continue his studies.

1938 Gains a PhD in just eighteen months and returns to King's, where he's recruited by the Government Code and Cipher School (GC&CS) and trained on Enigma.

1939 Reports to Bletchley Park the day after war is declared. Breaks the indicator system of Enigma, invents "Banburismus" and designs the Bombe.

1940 The first Bombe, "Victory", is installed at Bletchley, quickly followed by "Agnus Dei".

1941 Breaks the naval Enigma for the first time.

1942 Invents "Turingismus", also known as "Turingery", which is to be key in the workings of Colossus, the world's first electronic fixed-program computer. Sent to America to study American encryption.

1943 Invents the "Delilah" speech encryption machine.

1945 Joins the National Physics Laboratory to design the world's first electronic stored-program computer, called the "ACE", going head to head in a race with old colleague, Max Newman, in Manchester.

1946 Awarded the OBE for "wartime services".

1946–47 Gives a series of important lectures in London on computer design, attended by the designer of the Manchester "Baby" computer, Tom Kilburn.

1947 Gives earliest known lecture to mention what we now call "artificial intelligence".

1948 Narrowly misses out on a place at the Olympics for long-distance running due to leg injury. Quits NPL after a series of hold-ups on the ACE and joins Max Newman in Manchester to work on the Manchester Baby. Publishes the paper, *Intelligent Machinery*.

1950 Publishes a paper called *Computing Machinery and Intelligence*, proposing an "imitation game" (what we now call the "Turing test") to see if a computer can "think".

1951 Elected Fellow of the Royal Society.

1952 Publishes *The Chemical Basis of Morphogenesis*, anticipating what we now call "artificial life".

1952 Arrested and convicted.

1954 Dies in apparent suicide at home in Manchester.

1974 Bletchley "secrets" are declassified and the truth begins to come out, revealing Alan's role as a wartime hero.

2009 British government apologizes for its treatment of Alan.

2013 Queen issues a royal pardon.

2017 The Alan Turing law comes into being, pardoning men who were convicted of breaking old laws on homosexuality.

ALAN'S PALS

Alan wasn't the only brilliant mind in his story. A whole cast of characters played important parts.

Christopher Morcom (1911–1930)

Alan's childhood friend, Christopher, inspired Alan even after his untimely death. Just months before he died, Christopher had won a place at Cambridge University, at the same time as Alan was rejected. Determined to follow in Christopher's footsteps, Alan re-applied to Cambridge and was awarded a scholarship at King's. Before he left to take up his place, Alan also won Sherborne School's "Morcom Prize" for science twice.

Max Newman (1897–1984)

Alan first met Max at Cambridge, where one of Max's lectures inspired Alan to write the ground-breaking paper proposing a Universal Machine.

They went on to work together at Bletchley, where Max headed up the team that built Colossus. Then, after the war when Alan became frustrated with his own computing project, the ACE, Max offered Alan a job in Manchester to work on his version. Alan became a close friend of Max and his family.

Gordon Welchman (1906–1985)

A fellow Cambridge maths scholar (though at Trinity not King's), Gordon Welchman joined Alan at Bletchley to break Enigma. Together they worked on designing the Bombe, and it was Gordon's ingenious suggestion of the "diagonal board" that meant the machine could work quickly enough to decipher messages in time for troops to take action. After the war, he followed Hugh Alexander to become Head of Research for John Lewis, before travelling to America's top science university, Massachusetts Institute of Technology (MIT), to teach their first ever computing course. In 1982, three years before he died, he published a book called *The Hut Six Story: Breaking the Enigma Codes.*

Tommy Flowers (1905–1988)

An engineer for the General Post Office (GPO), Tommy was Alan's go-to man for any big project. He designed and built the Colossus, then worked with Alan on the design of the ACE. He was awarded the OBE in 1943. After the war, he applied for a loan to build another machine like Colossus but was turned down because the bank, unaware of his wartime work, didn't believe it could possibly work. Instead, he returned to working for the GPO, pioneering work on all-electronic telephone exchanges.

Joan Clarke (1917–1996)

Joan worked with Alan in Hut 8 and briefly became his fiancée. In honour of her crucial work on Enigma, she was awarded an MBE in 1946. She went on to work for GCHQ. Like many of his Bletchley colleagues, she remained friends with Alan until his death.

Alfred Dillwyn "Dilly" Knox (1884–1943)

A former King's scholar in classics, Dilly first worked for the government on code-cracking in World War One. At the end of that war, he joined GC&CS. He also went back to classics, damaging his eyesight when studying papyrus fragments (a form of codebreaking itself) at the British Museum. That didn't stop his secret work though. In the run-up to World War Two, along with Commander Dennison, he met the Poles for the handover of their Enigma documents before becoming chief cryptanalyst at Bletchley – so, Alan's boss. There he cracked the Italian Enigma (which didn't use a plugboard), using his own method called "rodding", but quickly became ill and had to start working from home instead. He died in 1943.

Robin Gandy (1919–1995)

Robin had been studying maths at King's College, Cambridge, for just two years when he enlisted for military service in 1940, and joined the National Physics Lab, where he was to meet and even live with Alan. Alan later supervised his PhD and they remained friends until Alan's death.

Fred Clayton (1912–1999)

Alan's friend from King's, Fred had been to visit Germany in 1937, witnessing the horrors of Nazism for himself. That led him to sponsor a Jewish refugee boy and encourage Alan to do the same. He also went to work at Bletchley Park, making good use of his fluent German, before being despatched to India to work on cracking

Japanese codes. After the war, he married the daughter of a family he'd stayed with in Dresden and went on to become a university professor. Although Clayton felt his eventual academic career suffered because of the war, Turing described him as "the most learned man I ever met".

QUIZ

Test your Alan facts with this quiz (don't worry, it's easier than cracking Enigma).

1. What was Alan's invented word for the sound made by seagulls fighting over food?

2. What was Alan's father's name?

3. Where did Alan's first foster parents live?

4. What was the name of Alan's best friend at Sherborne?

5. What was the name of Alan's teddy bear?

6. What instrument did Alan take up at Cambridge?

7. Which American university did Alan attend to do his PhD?

8. Which Roman leader has a cipher named after him?

9. Arthur Scherbius patented which cryptographic invention?

10. How many silver ingots did Alan bury?

11. What was the name of Alan's one-time fiancée?

12. Who did Alan write to, demanding more funding for Bombes?

13. What was the name of the ship that Alan took home from America during the war?

14. What colour was the cat adopted by Alan and Robin Gandy?

15. Which Olympics was Alan nearly in the running for?

16. What was the name of Alan's house in Wilmslow?

17. Which children's author used to go running with Alan?

18. Which children's books might have inspired Alan's interest in morphogenesis?

19. Where did Alan keep his OBE?

20. Where is the statue of Alan sitting on a bench with an apple in his hand?

ANSWERS

Binary Code
256
01001010
01100111
00011001
10
47
169

Caesar Shift
ALAN TURING ATE AN APPLE A DAY
ALAN HAD A BEAR CALLED PORGY

Vigenère Square
TNKIPQMIEQTNM

Answers to Quiz

1. Quockling
2. Julius
3. St Leonard's-on-Sea
4. Christopher Morcom
5. Porgy
6. Violin
7. Princeton
8. Caesar
9. Enigma
10. Two
11. Joan Clarke
12. Winston Churchill
13. *Empress of Scotland*
14. Ginger
15. London 1948
16. Hollymeade
17. Alan Garner
18. Kipling's *Just So Stories*
19. In his toolbox
20. Manchester

GLOSSARY

ACE: Alan's version of a stored-program electronic computer

Banburismus: Alan's method to crack the naval Enigma using holes punched in sheets of paper

Billet: living quarters assigned to a person

Binary: a way of writing numbers using only "1" and "0"

Bombe: Alan's and Gordon Welchman's machine that checked possible Enigma settings

Caesar shift: a monoalphabetic key that swaps letters by shunting the alphabet along by a stated number of places

Cipher: a way of writing a secret message by swapping one letter for another

Code: a way of writing a secret message by swapping one word for another

Colossus: the first computer, built to check settings on the *Lorenz* cipher

Crib: a "cheat" used to check for frequently used words in cipher text

Cryptanalyst: someone who works on cracking ciphers

Delilah: Alan's speech-encryption machine

Dolphin: German naval Enigma messages

Decipher/decrypt: to solve a secret message using a cipher

Encipher/encrypt: to make a secret message using a cipher

GC&CS: the Government Code and Cipher School, based at Bletchley Park

GCHQ: Government Communication Headquarters (the new version of GC&CS)

Key: the rule for encrypting a message

Lamp board: the part of the Enigma machine that lit up to show the encrypted or decrypted letter

Manchester Baby: the world's first stored-program electronic computer

Manchester Mark 1: the second version of the Baby, programmed by Alan

Meccano: a children's toy consisting of a set of metal and plastic components for making mechanical models

Morphogenesis: the process of biological growth and change

Newton, Isaac: an English mathematician and physicist who discovered gravity and is considered one of the most influential scientists of all time

Pinch: the capture of vital papers or equipment from the Germans

Plugboard: a set of sockets and jacks on Enigma to swap letters over

Public school: a private fee-paying secondary school

Reflector: part of the Enigma at the end of the wheels that "sent" a letter back through the wheels to change it several more times

Teleprinter: a device for transmitting telegraph messages as they are keyed, and for printing messages received

Traffic: the messages sent by machine

Tunny: the British name for the *Lorenz* cipher

Turingismus or Turingery: Alan's method for cracking Tunny

Turing test: a test to see if a computer can convince a judge it's a human

Universal Machine: Alan's imaginary machine that became the blueprint for computers

WRENS: women working for the Women's Royal Naval Service

Y station: radio stations that intercepted German messages

Yanks: referring to people from the United States of America

INDEX